Roaring Sil

Roaring Silence

Michael Clarke

Paul H. Crompton Ltd.
London

1st edition 1987
New edition 1994

London: Paul H. Crompton Ltd.
102 Felsham Road, Putney, London SW15 1DQ

New York: Talman Company
131 Spring Street, New York, N.Y. 10012, U.S.A.

Printed and bound in Great Britain by
Caric Print Ltd.
Clerwood, Corunna Main,
Andover, Hants SP10 1JE
(0264) 354887

FOREWORD

Karate is many things to many people. It may be studied seriously and even be lived as a way of life or merely practised from time to time for leisure. As a means of keeping fit it provides a well balanced and interesting exercise. Most students (not all), however, are attracted to Karate as a system of self defence.

In my opinion, Karate is greatly misunderstood by the public due mainly to the sensational type of press and demonstrations showing how, with one blow a pile of bricks is smashed. A common question asked of Karate-ka (Karate practitioners) is 'How many bricks can you break?'

This is the story of one man's encounter with Karate and the effect it has had on his life. It may seem a paradox to the uninitiated but there are many such stories of gentleness flowing from the practice of this seemingly violent art. The reader will see how the practice of Karate has played a part in saving the author from what might be termed by some as a wasted life. It is my hope that this may have a positive influence on those practitioners who are looking for more than mere physical exercise.

James Rousseau

I dedicate this book to my parents who have always been there whenever I was in need, and were my first teachers of life.

The author (1) with Aikman Sensei at the last training session before he went to become head of Norwegian Shukokai.

Further reading

In keeping with the principles of Goju-ryu, that is that we should understand the relationships of opposites to understand the whole, I have included a list of books for further reading. I do this because it will help to provide you with material for mental development as well as physical.

Karate-do – Chojiro Tani
Martial Arts, Traditions, History, People – John Corcoran and Emil Farkas
Karate-do Kyohan – Gichin Funakoshi
Classical Bujutsu, Classical Budo and Modern Bujutsu and Budo – Donn F. Draeger
Traditional Karate-do – Morio Higaonna
The Way of the Warrior – Howard Reid and Michael Croucher
Chinese Soft Exercise – Paul Crompton
Karate, Beginner to Black Belt – Henri D. Plee
The Fighting Arts – Choosing the Way – David Scott and Mick Pappas
Uechi-ryu Karate-do – Classical Chinese Okinawan Self Defence – George E. Mattson
Moving Zen – C. W. Nicol
Karate-do My Way of Life – Gichin Funakoshi
Karate-do – Nakaya
Karate History and Traditions – Bruce A. Haines

ACKNOWLEDGEMENTS

I would like to acknowledge the help I have received from my wife Kathy, whose help and encouragement gave me the confidence to write this book.

Also I would like to thank Paul Crompton for transforming my manuscript into an intelligible piece of literature.

And lastly I thank most sincerely my seniors and contemporaries in Karate for the help, guidance and friendship they have given and continue to give.

"Karate is the study of human relations". . . . .Higaonna Morio Sensei.

PREFACE

In this book I have told the story of the experiences, both good and bad, that I have had during my study of Karate-Do. It is evident from chapter one that had I not found Karate-Do when I did I would have inevitably travelled further along a path or way of life that would have left my life ruined.

I have tried to show the paradox that is all Martial arts, and how with the right guidance one can learn from, and accept, what at first seems to be at best a disjointed concept.

When I began to write this book I wanted only to relate my limited progress in Karate-Do so far. I wanted to do so without offending or embarrassing anyone. However the way Karate seems to be organized today I doubt if I have succeeded.

Throughout the text I have endeavoured to tell things as they were, or at least as I saw them. I hope my story will entertain, but also I hope it will in some small way enlighten.

For those who come after me on the difficult road of Martial Arts training I hope it will highlight some of the many pitfalls that await the novice student.

I know now that as a Shodan I stood only at the gateway to knowledge. However there are many things that can stop one from passing through. Pride, greed, temper, impatience and ego, will and do stop progress.

There are many different ways within the Martial Arts but

11

all have one thing in common, truth. If you are true to yourself from the beginning you will deviate little from the pathway that leads to real knowledge. It is well to remember that although there may be short cuts within the physical side of Martial Arts training, there are none when it comes to the attainment of real knowledge and ability.

I have found it impossible to relate everything I have experienced since I began to practice Karate-Do. However I hope I have included all the major landmarks of my journey.

This then is my story, make of what you will.

I have decided to include a short list of key words for the benefit of those who do not study Karate, or who have done so for only a short time.

Dojo

A dojo in Japan or on Okinawa is a place set aside for the learning of something. Do in Japanese translates as way, and so a Do-jo is a place where you learn to follow a way. This can be a way of dancing, making tea, or as in this case Karate.

Sensei

Although the word Sensei is commonly used, it is in my opinion misused on most occasions. Translated simply as 'Teacher' the word holds much more meaning than merely someone who gives lessons in a particular subject. Rather it implies by the characters used to write the word in Japanese that someone called Sensei is of a true, pure, and honest nature. Also that this person has travelled this way before you and is therefore in a position to help and guide you through the lessons you are now learning.

Kyu/Dan

This ranking system is fairly new to Karate, and still causes some discussion amongst traditionalists as to its relavence within the study of Karate. Nevertheless it is well established now throughout the world. Basically, the term 'Kyu' is given to grades in Karate below that of the Black Belt. The different Kyu grades are shown by way of different colours of belt. Although these colours vary from system to system in general they all start with the first grade as White and the last Kyu grade as brown. The number of Kyu grades also differs from style to style.

The Black Belt grades move upward from First Dan to as high as Tenth Dan. In all these grades the holder wears a Black Belt. Although there is a trend in the USA for people over fifth Dan to wear Red and White belts. It should be pointed out however that these grades are not inter-changeable, and there exists today such varying standards that one really has to see a person doing Karate to assess his or her ability.

Techniques

Here is a list covering some of the Japanese terms used for Karate techniques.

Zuki – Punch.	Oi – Front.	Jodan – High
Geri – Kick.	Gyaku – Reverse.	
Uke – Block.	Mae – Forward.	Chudan – Middle
Dachi – Stance.	Mawashi – Swinging around from the side.	Gedan – Low
Uchi – Strike.	Barai – Sweep	

I hope this short list will be helpful to you to understand some of the techniques described later. You should be able to fit some of the words together and come up with a recognisable technique, e.g. Mae (front) Geri (kick) Maegeri (front kick)

Ryu

Ryu translates as 'School', and in this context is used to describe the various schools or styles of Karate. For example the Goju-Ryu – the Hard-Gentle School of Karate. Since its popularization in Japan and later in the west there are now literally thousands of different schools and styles of Karate. However on Okinawa there still remain the two main systems of Karate from which all these sprang.

Nunchaku

This weapon, made famous by the late Bruce Lee, was in fact in use for many hundreds of years throughout the east. Nunchaku on Okinawa form part of what is known as Ko-Budo, the study of weapons systems for the purpose of combat. However in our days Ko-Budo is taught in the same way as Karate-do, that is to say as a way of improving oneself through hard and diligent study.

Hojo-Undo

'Supplementary Training'. This is something most schools on Okinawa still practice. Although for the most part this has been dropped by the western Karate-ka. This kind of training involves training with various weights that are designed to build strong grip, and strengthen your arms. Also there are devices to punch, strike, and kick, and one, the Kongo-Ken, which Miyagi Sensei brought back with him from his stay on Hawaii, which is used to wrestle with. It is the Makiwara

14

punching board that is probably the best known of all these tools. Placed in the ground and firm enough to withstand constant punching, the Makiwara is in my opinion the best single tool to help improve a Karate-ka's power, stance, and mind. It is, I feel, a must for every serious Karate man, and I bitterly regret missing out on this kind of training in my early days.

As a foot note, the Makaiwara was at one time on Okinawa a focus for social occasions Men would meet in each other's backyards in the evenings and have a good old pound at the Makiwara. Many of these men never took Karate lessons, formal or otherwise, however they recognised the necessity of having a strong punch should they ever be attacked by robbers.

In the Dojo of Uehara Sensei on Okinawa there stands at the back two Makiwara. This is quite usual in a Goju-ryu Dojo, however one of these Makiwara differs from all others that I have seen. The difference lies in the small device Sensei Uehara has fixed to the back wall behind the board. For hanging there he has a small brass plumb line. The small weight can be moved closer or further from the back of the Makiwari and the idea is to hit the board hard enough to strike the weight and set it swinging. On the occasion I visited Uehara Dojo I was invited to try and set the weight swinging. I tried but without much success. Even with the weight just behind the board I could with my best punch just touch the target. Sensei Uehara on the other hand had no such trouble, and in fact moved the weight back to what seemed an impossible distance, and from there still managed to strike the weight so hard as to make it hit the back wall with tremendous power. It sounded like someone hitting the wall with a hammer.

On returning to England I met someone else who had trained at Uehara Dojo, Bill Cuzzocrea. He confirmed Uehara Sensei's tremendous punching ability. He also told me that he too was invited to 'Have a go'. The result was he split his knuckle trying to move that elusive brass ball.

The author taking part in a Bo, (long staff) course in Manchester, 1977, taught by Aikman Sensei.

Chapter 1

I was born in the upstairs front bedroom of 88, Kylemore Drive, Dublin, on Saturday, May 14th, 1955. I was the fifth child of six, all of whom grew up to be strong and healthy. However, I was the only one to follow in the footsteps of my father and become a pugilist. he had been an amateur boxer as a boy and continued boxing well into his twenties. During the second world war he worked in London as an engineer and often used some of his work activities to help him in his training. He told me how he had once dressed up in two pairs of overalls, a large sweater and a balaclava before climbing inside a large boiler and cleaning it out. He did this to make himself sweat and lose weight for a forthcoming fight. It had the desired effect, but how my father fared on that occasion I really don't know. He often told me of his fights, not all of which were in the ring. After the war he returned to Dublin to marry my mother. Work was not so plentiful in Ireland, and in 1956 my father and his now growing family moved to Manchester. I was eight months old.

As a schoolboy I was rarely if ever involved in fights. But soon after I left school at the age of fifteen I began to get involved in street fights. This was not entirely my own fault, and the first year I never once started a fight myself. Life in a large city like Manchester has always presented problems for teenagers and in 1969 the cult known as the Skinheads became fashionable amongst the working class youth of the day. By the time I left school a year later they were well established. The idea was to look as tough and menacing as possible, and to this end youths would bleach their jeans white, wear high level boots called Doc Martins and, perhaps the most startling of all, have their heads completely shaved.

Of course, looking tough does not mean that you are tough, and so it was always important to find safety in numbers by belonging to a gang. The two main gangs in Manchester at the time were the Hulme Team and the Wythenshawe Crew. One of my elder brothers was a leader of the Hulme Team and although I never actually joined a gang I acquired some notoriety because of the reputation of my brother. In some situations this was advantageous but in others in fact it was downright dangerous! From time to time I was confronted simply because of who my brother was. Fortunately for me I always came out on top. These fights and the results served as a flame to others and they came to me like moths to try their arm, or rather their fists and feet. It was just like the tradition of the old Wild West, seeing who was fastest on the draw. In the space of one year I had over one hundred fights, and so by the age of sixteen I was considered to be a veteran.

By the beginning of 1972 I had developed a strong taste for fighting, and so I embarked on an even more intense diet of conflict. Every weekend I could be found fighting in some club, pub or just in the street. Inevitably this kind of conduct led me into trouble with the police and my parents. A trail of fights and court appearances followed, ending in the Manchester Crown Court. The incident which brought me there had been inspired by three youths who had set upon and beaten up the retarded brother of one of my friends. I wreaked such vengeance on them that charges of Grievous Bodily Harm, Assault and Battery and A.B.H. were levelled against me. The judge said that it was a case of misplaced loyalty and hoped that by imposing a two year Borstal sentence on me I would be able to ponder on my life to date and the direction it was going. In retrospect I will be forever grateful to him for my time spent in Strangeways Prison and Hindley Borstal did indeed give me much time to think and realise the stupidity of my lifestyle.

For the first time since leaving school I was forced to do physical exercise and after reaching a high level of fitness in a relatively short time I began to enjoy my three workouts a week. Although I had resolved to keep myself to myself, conflict was inevitable. The first part of my sentence was served in Strangeways prison, and during my time there I had two very unpleasant experiences. The first took place within an hour of my arrival. In the centre of the cell blocks a large area of the floor is covered by a heavy iron grille. In the middle of the grille is a table on which are the books containing a register of all the inmates, and also the orders of the day for the prison officers. I arrived at the cell block from the induction centre and with all the things I had gone through that day I was feeling very low. When the huge studded gates banged closed behind me I had the most vivid impression of really entering a prison and I wondered if I would ever be free again. I was handed over to an officer who stood next to the table in the centre of the grille.

He immediately began to shout at me, calling me names, and generally making the most of my evident, huge burden of loneliness and sense of captivity. When he saw that he was not having the desired effect, since I was as low as I could be already and nothing a bastard like him could say would have made me feel any lower, he finally screamed, 'Come here you little sod!' His vocabulary of insults exhausted he watched me as I approached him, then suddenly stepped forward and hit me hard with his left fist, in the face. The blow sent me sprawling across the floor. The bedding I had been holding fell all around me. He went on with the words, 'Pick up your things, Clarke, and don't ever step on this grille again; it's out of bounds to all scum like you, understand!' The last word was delivered with all the force of his vocal chords. Of course I had not known about the rule of not stepping on the grille and he had lured me on to it deliberately. Whilst this incident took place everyone else carried on about their business as if nothing unusual was happening and it made me realise that I was alone, and that the best thing for me to do was to keep my nose clean, as best I could.

The second event took place during my last week at Strangeways. As I had been convicted of a violent crime I was not permitted to share a cell, and so I was forced into solitary confinement for up to sixteen hours a day. Whilst I was sitting in my cell awaiting cell inspection one day the door swung open and in came two prison officers. I was ordered to stand in a corner facing the wall and from there I heard the two men begin to ransack the cell. They said they were looking for hidden weapons or drugs. A kick in the back of the leg told me that the search was over. I was told to clean the cell up as it would be inspected for cleanliness in five minutes, that should the cell fail the inspection I would be disciplined, and so on, but I managed to clean the cell in time and did not get disciplined. It was only after four and a half weeks that I was transferred to Hindley Closed Borstal.

My time there was by and large incident free. However, I did have one fight soon after my arrival, but to be honest it was not my fault. Along with twenty or so other inmates I was waiting to be assessed for work. The interviews were taking place in the education wing, and so we were all sitting in a classroom waiting for our turns. In the desk in front of me was a particularly childish individual from Liverpool. He was everything I hated in people; weak, dirty, full of spots, and latching on to any individual or group who would tolerate him. True to form he instigated a spitting contest which turned into a free for all with idiots spitting at one another from all directions. It was not long before this character was hit on the side of the face by a particularly thick green gob of spit. He turned on me, convinced that I had spat at him. He began to threaten me with his friends and described in detail what they were going to do to me. I had heard this kind of boastful threat before and so it made no impression on me. He then made the enormous mistake of calling me a bastard. In those days I already had an extremely short temper anyway, but if there was one word guaranteed to start me fighting it was that one. His right hand was over the side of the desk in front of me so I lifted my right knee up to my chest and brought down my heel in a stamp on to his hand. His scream could be heard all over the Borstal. I had followed the kick through, knocking the desk over, and was standing holding him up by the hair when two officers burst into the room. They stopped the almost certain carnage which would have followed, for once my temper was aroused I had little or no control over it and often only stopped after a lot of damage had been done. As I had broken three of the lad's fingers I was sentenced to ten days in the punishment block. This meant being locked up for twenty-three hours a day. A bright orange light was kept on at all times, day and night, and needless to say the accompanying discipline was extremely tough. I was released from Borstal on December 13th 1973 having served only eight months of my two year sentence in custody. The remainder was served under a probationary order. As you can imagine, with all the regular hours and exercise I was in very good condition physically. After my release I discovered that a few of my friends had started training in Karate, and one night following some discussion I decided I would go with them to their lesson the following Tuesday. So it was that on January 29th 1974 I began my training in Karate.

21

The first training session with Tomiyama Sensei, as he explains about the exchange of bodyweight when punching. Author's head in top right corner.

Chapter 2

I can well remember coming home after that first night of training, tired and soaked with sweat. A lot of people were trying Martial Arts in those days. Bruce Lee was all the rage, and dojos or training halls up and down the country were bursting at the seams with new members. I had missed all the fuss made over Bruce Lee whilst I was 'away' and consequently I often felt out of place listening to my fellow beginners raving over his exploits on and off the screen. I had begun my training in Karate for two reasons: to maintain my high level of fitness and to make sure that my friends and associates could not beat me in a fight. Remember that I saw myself as a tough fighter who, after all, had only been beaten twice in over two hundred fights. I took to training like a duck to water, that is to say my mind did. The idea of fighting, the discipline that ran through the club, these things were strong attractions to me. However my body was finding it quite difficult to fit into the unaccustomed rules and regulations. These included correct posture, balance, weight application and so on. In addition to these there was the awareness training, correct application and so on and so on, distancing and timing and many other things which I had never dreamed of before. I saw people whom I would have thought of as easy to fight move with incredible accuracy when punching and kicking. Some of the kicks I had never even imagined, much less seen before.

Six weeks later I took my first grading and passed. I was now graded 8th kyu, in the Shukokai Karate Union. It was Saturday, 13th March, 1974. At last I felt that I had achieved something positive in my life. No more red beginner's tabs on my belt ran through my mind. In those days I was very conscious of the colour of my belt and the prestige that the various grades carried.

That summer I travelled with other members of my dojo to Rotherham in Yorkshire to witness my first Karate tournament. This was the Shukokai Karate Union's 1974 Northern Championships. This annual event already had a terrible reputation. Stories were told of veritable blood baths when the higher grades got going and it was said that only the very brave or the very stupid entered the contests. Despite this awesome reputation the competition always attracted a very high entry. The percentage of stupid or brave or neither I do not know. This year was no exception to the rule. It was the first time that I had seen Karate of such a high standard from people other than my own instructor. Here I also witnessed fighting the like of which I had never seen before. Black Belts fought one another with tremendous speed and skill. In both the individual and team events they fought with precision and agression.

The event that I remember most vividly was the team contest between Manchester and Sheffield. My friends and I were of course giving our support to the Manchester team; not only because they were our home team but because our own instructor was a member of the team and this was our first chance to see him pit his skills against those of his contemporaries. The whole contest was full of hard, fast fighting, but sometimes it was just a little bit too hard and the end result was a win for Sheffield. This was because the Manchester team were disqualified one after the other for excessive contact. Yes, indeed, the fighting at Rotherham was not for the weak in spirit.

I recall also the wonderful demonstrations given by the top Dan grades of the association such as Stan Knighton, Eddie Daniels, and Butch White. It was also on this occasion that I saw a Japanese performing Karate for the first time. His name was Tomiyama Keiji. (The second name is given first in Japanese custom.) He was a twenty-four year old Yondan, the guest of honour, and he performed his favourite kata, Sanchin. I was very impressed by his obvious skill, but never guessed at the time the importance that he was to have in my future Karate development. The following weekend I found myself standing once again in front of Roy Stanhope, 4th Dan. In those days he was the chief instructor for Shukokai in England, and conducted all the gradings in the Manchester area. I cannot remember much about my early gradings but I was successful in this one and rose to the rank of 7th kyu. At last, I thought to myself, I am beginning to climb the ladder of colours to Black Belt.

The club I had joined was called the Ming-Chuan Karate Club, and it had its headquarters in Ashton-under-Lyne, some few miles from Manchester. My friends and I trained at the Didsbury dojo about ten miles from Ashton, in the suburbs of Manchester. At Disbury there were about fifty students, mostly beginners like me, or low ranking students. There were a few higher graded students and I can remember two Brown Belts in particular and the difference in attitude which they had to the lower grades. The most senior had the grade of 1st Kyu, the next grade down from Black Belt and the fact that I cannot even recall his name gives you some idea of the relevance he had to my Karate career. He was full of his own importance and had little time for anyone else except the instructor whom he fawned on and crept up to at every available opportunity.

Not long after I had passed my 7th kyu grading he began to instruct at the Tuesday class, in the evening. This was because our instructor had so many life commitments that it made Tuesday evenings almost impossible for him. On one notable evening he called everyone together, made us kneel, seiza, and began to read us a letter. He told us that it was from Mr. Stanhope. I cannot remember the exact words but the gist of it was that we were to train in future only with this 1st kyu who was taking the class and that we were to have nothing further to do with our instructor. I for one was confused and as I sat there listening to him reading out complaint after complaint about our instructor I began to wonder about the validity of what was taking place. After the lesson, as my friends and I were walking home we discussed the evening's events. I did not like this Brown Belt, 1st Kyu, nor did I trust him. Even if Mr. Stanhope was a 4th Dan, not even he was going to tell me who I could train with and not train with. My good friend John Carey and I resolved to approach our instructor and try to sort something out with him. We saw him. It was the first and only time that I saw him lose his temper.

The matter had what I considered to be the correct conclusion. The Brown Belt was expelled from the S.K.U. The letter was proved to be a hoax, a fabrication from an over active imagination; what is more, the same man even forged Mr. Stanhope's signature from his licence. I was destined to meet this man some years later in very different circumstances.

The second Brown Belt's name was Mike and he held 3rd Kyu grade. He impressed me greatly with his positive attitude, discipline and knowledge of technique. He was a short, chubby man in his early thirties. My first meeting with him came on my very first night of training. After Mokuso, several minutes of silent sitting, which preceded every training session, the students split up into two groups – beginners and graded.

Mike would almost always take charge of the beginners and so from day one they would be subject to discipline and hard work. As I progressed he was always there to show me something new, but the thing I gained most from Mike were the insights into the etiquette of Karate and the importance of paying attention to detail, as he always did.

By now I was itching to put my newly learned and still limited skills to the test. The opportunity came when three Shukokai dojo plus our own got together to have a friendly competition. We arrived early at the dojo of the Collichurst Karate Club and to our surprise there were people packing the place, all around the fighting area. We soon changed into our gi's, karate uniforms, and began to warm up. The fighting order had been made up and I was drawn against the only woman in the competition for my first fight. My friend John fought the first bout for our team and won, and then I found myself standing opposite a woman opponent. Needless to say I felt very confident of the outcome but was I in for a shock. The referee started the contest and I jumped forward with a maegeri, front kick. It caught her hard in the stomach and she fell to the floor holding her body. The contest stopped for a little while but she was soon back on her feet though now plainly frightened of me. I did not receive any points for the kick but to be quite honest I was not even very sure as to what constituted a scoring technique anyway. I forced her backwards time and again into a corner. However, every time I did so I could not bring myself to hit her again. Time was running out. The crowd, led by our club supporters, were yelling at me to punch her. For one fatal moment I glanced across at my team mates and bang! – she hit me full in the stomach with a strong reverse punch. I felt sick. I just could not believe it. The referee called us back to the starting points, announced the woman's score and re-started the contest. The time keeper waited just five seconds and called time.

As I sat down I was already thinking of giving up karate! After all, I said to myself, I can fight with the best of them but as soon as rules and regulations are introduced, well, imagine me being beaten in a fight by a woman, a girl . . . My ego had just taken a massive blow. This seemed even worse, when, at the end of the first round, I had been the only member of our team to lose. With the overall score standing at four wins to one in our favour we moved on to fight the winners of the other match.

The team we faced seemed formidable to us. They were all from the Ardwick dojo and were all green belt students of Mr. Stanhope, and to no one's surprise we were beaten. But we were beaten by only the smallest of margins, a mere half point. By the end of the contests I was feeling much happier, not having given up Karate in the interim, because I had beaten my opponent who was an experienced green belt. This win did not stop my father from laughing at me and teasing me later on when I told him what had happened.

Some weeks later I was asked to take part in a demon-stration with members of our main dojo in Ashton. The part I played in the event was simple enough. All I had to do was to perform 'ippon-kumite', pre-arranged one-step sparring, with a fellow 7th kyu. We trained diligently at it for weeks and finally the day arrived. The audience numbered hundreds and my partner became more and more nervous with every passing minute. He was so nervous in the end that when we stood up to do our part his usual controlled actions were forgotten and he hit me full power with an elbow strike to the back. The blow damaged my right shoulder blade and forced me to rest from training for three weeks.

After my enforced lay off which I hated I soon got back into the routine of training once again. Two months later I got a second chance to try my luck in competition. The occasion was the Manchester inter-club challenge. It was open to Kyu grades only and attracted entries from all over the Greater Manchester area. I do not remember how many teams took part but I do remember that our team were disqualified for being too aggressive. The incident stands out vividly in my mind. We had won our first contest and were feeling very positive. It had been decided that we would reverse our order of fighting for the second round. This meant that I would be fighting last. By the time that it was my turn we were in a tricky situation. This was because the first four bouts had resulted in two wins for each team. It was therefore up to me to win my own bout so that we could go through to the third round. Our opponents were from Warrington and made up of Brown Belts. This did not bother me as I had already won one fight and recently been promoted to 6th Kyu so I was feeling confident. As the referee started the contest the Brown Belt rushed towards me with an Oi-zuki, lunge punch, to the face. I stepped back with my right foot while at the same time blocking the punch with my left handed Shuto-uke or open palm block. As I stepped back my toe had been forced down and back under my foot. It was my big toe and the pain shot through me, my temper rising. The Brown Belt had committed himself completely with his lunge punch and although it was blocked his body continued forward carrying the two of us tumbling out of the fighting area and into the crowd.

I was furious. My toe was throbbing like mad and I felt nauseous. The referee called us back to the starting lines and we began to fight again. This time I leaped forward, yelling like a mad man. I kicked my opponent full in the bladder with my sore foot and as he doubled over I brought my right fist down hard on the side of his head. Obviously I had lost control, and the referee pulled me off and threw me back to the side of the fighting area. The Brown Belt was brought back to his feet, shaken and dazed. He elected to carry on, and after the referee had given me an official warning he

29

resumed the contest. I immediately repeated the attack and this time my opponent's nose caught the full impact of my punch. It burst like a ripe tomato, blood going everywhere. I felt vindicated. Uproar broke out all over the place and the referee disqualified me. However at the time I cared little for the result. I had a great big smile on my face because this was the first real fight I had had for years. These thoughts passed through my mind and though in all honesty I should not have, I felt marvellous. My brother, who had witnessed all this, sat there looking puzzled. 'What do you think?' I asked him. 'You're mad,' he replied, 'I thought you had to show control!' My response was brief. I said, 'I did, he's still breathing isn't he?' As you can see from my comments, I still had a long way to go.

(Left to right) Dave Milward, Tomiyama Sensei, Suzuki Sensei, Vickers Sensei, and author.

Chapter 3

Because of the quick turnover of students at our dojo my instructor would occasionally ask me to show the beginners the first few moves in their training. I was now training very hard; the Karate bug had bitten me well, and I was in its power. On Sunday mornings my friend John and I would go to Ardwick Sports Centre in Manchester. In those days a Kung fu class was held in the main gym upstairs. This was run by Mr. Danny Connors, and would always fill the entire area. I would watch the proceedings from behind the large curtain which divided off one part of the gym from the other. The Kung fu class ended at mid-day, after which other people could use the gym for a nominal fee. After listening to what Mr. Connors was teaching we would wait for the Karate Black Belts from all over Manchester who used the afternoon period to take private lessons. Most of them charged ridiculous fees and imparted very little knowledge to their pupils. Indeed I am sure that John and I were the ones who benefited most from the afternoon sessions as we listened to what each and every one of the Black Belts had to say. We copied the techniques from behind our cover. In all we used to spend about six hours there every Sunday, and by witnessing what took place we learned and progressed faster than we would have done had we spent our Sundays in some other way. We soaked up the atmosphere too, as well as the visible technical details.

I ended my first year of training as a 6th kyu. It had cost

me much in time, sweat and pain. For two months I had been training whilst suffering from an unguinal hernia. It began to show itself as a small lump at the very base of my torso, where my left leg joined my body. At first I told no one but it continued to grow and over the weeks became so large that I could push four fingers into my body. Finally I went to the doctor. He feared that it might develop into a strangulated hernia and made speedy arrangements for my admittance to hospital. The surgeon explained to me that the hole in my body was too large for it simply to be stitched together as was usually the case. Instead he proposed to insert a patch, made from rubber and I was told it would give me more mobility than if I did without it. I gave my permission for the operation and the surgeon went ahead. It was a complete success. Whilst I was in hospital I had been given a book written by Bruce A. Haines called 'Karate's History & Traditions'. For the first time I began to read about the many different forms of empty hand fighting that had originated in and close to Asia.

A few days after the operation I was reading the book when the surgeon came on to the ward to conduct his rounds. When he saw the book he asked about my interest in martial arts. I told him that I had been training for a year and that I was eager to get back into training again. He told me that in his opinion my involvement with Karate should end right then and there. He said that it would be quite mad of me to continue, in such a sport. I had never thought of Karate as a sport, but as something which I simply did and loved. Listening to the doctor calling it a sport somehow cheapened it and I thought to myself, this is no sport and I will carry on with it.

Five weeks later I lined up with the others once more in the dojo, ready to practice. To be honest I was not up to my usual standard but that was as much due to the six week lay off as to the operation. My training soon picked up and in the following months I passed two more grading exams, which brought me to 4th Kyu. About this time I also began to take a more active role in the running of the dojo. For instance I was now responsible for the calling of the attendance register and for collecting the training fees.

In October I attended my first residential course at the National Recreation Centre at Lillieshall. I went to the course along with another 4th Kyu from my dojo and as we drove down the motorway we wondered what we would experience on this our first such course. We arrived early on the Monday morning full of anticipation. The course was to run from Monday afternoon to Friday mid-day. There were four training sessions a day and each one was taken in turn by the four instructors who were running the course. The training was very hard but enjoyable. I noticed how many differences there were between students from various parts of the country. As I had only trained in Manchester it never occurred to me that there would be differences within the same style such as I saw here. I wondered how this could be, but when I investigated I found that it was not a new problem and indeed even today many associations are still trying to standardise their techniques. I awoke on Wednesday morning to find my friend's bed empty. He had risen early and without letting anyone know he had gone home. I couldn't believe it. Not only did he not tell me and leave me stranded, as it was his car we had driven down in, but he also left it to me to tell the instructors. I have never felt so embarrassed in my life.

That evening there was to be a friendly competition and everyone was asked if they would like to take part. I was most surprised to see the lack of interest amongst the karate-ka, karate students, and only twenty-five or so took part out of the hundred and fifty on the course. All but four of us were Black Belts. The competition came and went. It was no big deal. So, I wondered, why had so many people cowered away

33

from it? That night, the instructors bought everyone who had taken part a beer; a small 'prize' but it gave some feeling of recognition to the participants.

On the Thursday afternoon a grading was held and I lined up with the other 4th Kyu grades to attempt my Brown Belt. As the grading progressed I felt more and more confident. By the time I reached the fighting stage I felt great. I had two fights in which I had been the most dominant, or so I thought. The grading ended and I felt sure that I had passed. Everyone had to wait until the following day to get the results. This was the first time that I had felt confident about the outcome of a grading exam and it never even entered my head that I might fail. The instructors, led by Mr. Eddie Daniels, began to read out the names of those who had passed. Finally he came to me. 'Mr. Clarke?' 'Yes, Sensei,' I said with a big smile already beginning to crease my face. 'I'm sorry, Mr. Clarke, but you have failed. Please try again.' I could not believe my ears. I almost told them that they had got the wrong name. I was really quite devastated.

My instructor asked how I had got on. Though the expression of doom on my face must have told its own story. But he asked me anyway! That night he worked me to exhaustion, never giving me a chance to think about and dwell upon my recent grading, and feel sorry for myself. Instead, from the way he pushed me that night it was all I could do to stay on my feet. The following weekend he took me to Sheffield to train at the dojo of Mr. Stan Knighton. In fact it was an S.K.U. instructors' session but my instructor had obtained permission for me to attend it. This was a fantastic honour for me. There I was surrounded by the best Karate-ka of the association. I found it hard going at times, especially from the technical angle but it was a marvellous opportunity for me and I grasped it with both hands. These sessions were held once a month and in all I attended six of them. It was a big thrill to be training with people like Terry Potage, Ossie Rowe and on occasion with guests like Eugene Codrington.

It was due to this kind of extra guidance and help from my instructor that I began to progress, and by the time another grading came along I was ready for it. This time I was suffering from no illusions. It was December 14th 1975, and for me the promotion to 3rd Kyu was the best Christmas present I could have wished for.

Author (1) sparring with Fujiwara Toshio, a member of the Tani party, in 1980.

Tani Sensei, 8th dan, founder of Shukokai karate,
with the author in Leicester, 1980.

Chapter 4

Not long after my promotion to 3rd Kyu I had my first lesson with a Japanese instructor. I had always thought the Japanese were small, thin people but when I arrived in Bolton with my instructor for a lesson with Kimura Sensei I had all my preconceptions destroyed. Kimura Sensei turned out to be a big man, in every sense of the word. He is quite tall and is very broad. This was of course a surprise to me, but his Karate was everything I expected and hoped it would be, and more. This particular first lesson dealt with basic punching and kicking, and I also remember some very interesting practice on balance and body weight distribution.

I found Kimura Sensei to be a hard taskmaster. He seemed to have little patience with anyone who failed to grasp his theories. However, I did enjoy myself, though the lesson was hard; but at no time did I see him persecute a student as I have seen other Japanese instructors do. After the lesson he was easy to approach and eager to answer any questions put to him.

1976 was the year in which I began to take my training very seriously. My kicking, always a sore point, began to improve at this stage. I began to feel my techniques more, and because of that I started to understand Karate itself much better. It seemed as if my own Karate was taking a big leap forward. This was because my instructor changed the club's affiliation. He moved from the Shukokai Karate Union to the

Shukokai World Karate Union. Though I stay away from politics myself I think that some kind of explanation of this situation is necessary. To the best of my knowledge the following account of events is true and accurate.

In 1973, Mr. Tani, the Japanese founder of the Shukokai style of Karate, came to tour and hold friendly competitions in Britain. The S.K.U. had been asked to host the Japanese visitors but the executive committee declined this request. Because of this Mr. Bob Aikman who was the then secretary of the S.K.U. resigned his position as he believed in following the Japanese teaching and strengthening the bond between Japan and England, not cutting it. Along with five other dojo Mr. Aikman formed the Shukokai World Karate Union (England). This was then affiliated with the already existing S.W.K.U. Europe to Japan.

The new situation arose in which there were two separate groups representing Shukokai Karate in England, and both training in that style. As a face saving exercise which involved having a Japanese instructor connected to them the S.K.U. retained the services of Kimura Sensei, though within a few years they parted company with him, causing yet another split within their ranks. The S.W.K.U. England received their instruction from Suzuki Sensei and his team of Japanese instructors who were resident in Europe. Relationships between the two groups were to say the least strained. The S.K.U. had the all important official recognition by the then ruling body for Karate, the British Karate Control Commission, while the S.W.K.U.(E) were unrecognised, and therefore considered like many groups outside the present day M.A.C. to be cowboys.

However the S.W.K.U.(E) carried on, and by the following year, 1974, had grown sufficiently strong in membership to invite Mr. Tani and a university team over for another tour. It was hoped that after the visit arrangements could be made

38

to have a resident Japanese instructor in England. Although representations were made repeatedly through the correct channels the S.K.U. executive always managed to block any attempt to obtain a work permit. So although there were seven Japanese Sensei living in Europe, none were allowed to settle in England. Mr. Aikman and the other instructors who had formed the S.W.K.U.(E) all lived in and around the Midlands and we in the Northwest received very little news about all the commotion at the time. So much so that my own instructor was led to believe that Mr. Aikman had left the S.K.U. because of a discrepancy in his work as secretary and no more was heard of the split in our area until three years later. My instructor met an old friend of his who knew what had really happened and shortly after this meeting he contacted Mr. Aikman, and arranged to meet him at the S.W.K.U.(E) Championships in Peterborough.

A six man delegation from our dojo travelled down to Peterborough on September 19th. We walked into the main hall of a large new sports centre and watched Karate being performed to a very high standard. Everything seemed to be well organised. There were both empty hand and weapons kata being demonstrated in competition and the fighting was fast and furious. I liked what I saw immediately; but it wasn't up to me. The result of the meeting was that our dojos would join the S.W.K.U.(E) on a trial basis, as they were keen to maintain their high standards. We made the transition with little difficulty and for the next year and a half my instructor, fellow Brown Belt Dave Millard, and I spent three Sundays a month in Nottingham or Derby on squad training sessions. The boost in my Karate had come all right and I was now working for a place in the English team; believe me, work was the right word for it.

I gained a place in the team and one Friday in mid-November the English participants left with their supporters to take part in a tournament in Brussels, Belgium. The event was held in the Anderlecht stadium in the heart of the city and attracted an enormous crowd. I did fairly well and out of a total of ten fights was beaten only once. As well as fighting in the team and the individual events I was also in the Kata competition. In those days if you were lucky enough to be in the competition at all you entered as many events as possible. The Kata I chose to do was Sanchin. My nerves got the better of me and I added an extra Mawashi-uke movement on the end, so after all my practice and preparation I was eliminated in the first round!

I have been asked on various occasions what was the hardest blow I've ever had to take. I usually find this type of question hard to answer but in this case it comes easily. The most devastating punch I have ever had the misfortune to receive came in the individual competition at my first European Championships. I had been doing really well considering that I was only Brown Belt and most of my opponents were Dan grades, Black Belts. I had fought five times and won, but now I found myself opposite Mr. Bob Lord, 3rd Dan. Bob is a big man, standing over six feet tall, whereas your truly comes in at just five feet six. I knew Bob quite well from the squad training sessions and we had always got along really well. He had a reputation for being a hard hitter but I wasn't bothered about that at the time. I don't know what Bob had in mind as regards tactics but as the fight began I almost changed all his plans.

The referee was Mr. Tomiyama and as he began the fight Bob rushed towards me. I dropped down on one knee and punched him in the stomach. It took Bob right off his feet and he shot back three or four feet before landing on his backside. I remember to this day the shout that went up from the crowd. Everyone was amazed. But believe me I was the most amazed and even now I recognise that punch for what it was – sheer good luck. It was nothing more than a reflex action, but even so there I was after a few seconds in the lead, albeit by only a half point. The rest of the fight was uneventful until the last thirty seconds was called. Then Bob put me under pressure. I had decided that I was going to block and counter whatever he threw at me. He came forward kicking with his long legs. As I blocked one of his kicks he followed through with a punch that hit me right in the face. There was a blinding flash that took almost two minute(s) to clear and my ears were ringing and hissing. Blood covered my chin and began to fill my mouth. Mr. Tomiyama asked me if I was all right. 'Yes, yes, I'm o.k.' But of course I was not. The fight was restarted and I could see Bob coming towards me through the fog that clouded my vision. 'Yame'. Time had run out. I was saved. Bob would go through to the next round because he had been given a full point for his technique. The crowd booed. Bob got angry, but I was just glad that the day was over for me. It took a few days to recover fully from that punch and I still bear the scar to this day where one of my bottom front teeth came through the skin in my lower lip.

The next eighteen months seemed to fly by. I continued to represent the association and had some marvellous experiences. Towards the middle of 1977 I began to think about my Shodan grading and how I should prepare for it. On Sunday January 15th 1978 I entered a small church hall in Nottingham along with fifteen other hopefuls. It was 1.30 p.m. We emerged at 10.00 p.m. having completed a half hour written exam and a practical test which lasted eight hours. For those of us who passed it was a wonderful feeling of achievement and I was absolutely shattered into the bargain. I knew well the feeling of disappointment also, and my heart went out to those who had not been successful. It is indeed good to see, years later, many of those who had been unsuc-

41

cessful on that day now holding Dan grades within the association.

It is often the case when relying on memory to find that you have forgotten the bad or poor performances of the past and likewise always remember the highspots of byegone days. Also there is always the danger of exaggeration. People will tend to think that things were all so much harder in their day and this leads to a slight bending of the truth sometimes, and sometimes to downright lies. I have tried to avoid this in order that people in the future will get a true picture of what took place during my own progress in Karate. Tales of blood and gore always seem to go hand in hand with competitions in my early days but I was never aware of great injuries suffered in those days at the hands of fellow Karate-ka. However, that said, I was once in fact involved directly in what turned out quite badly for two of the other participants in an event.

The occasion was a return match between S.W.K.U. (E) and the S.W.K.U. (Scotland). It had been decided some months earlier that the two countries should meet twice a year for friendly competition, but the first meeting was, as far as friendly competiton goes, a disaster! Before the competition had run its course the whole thing had to be called to a halt. Tempers had become completely frayed and raw emotion had won the day over control and good judgement. Thankfully I had not been able, in the end, to make the trip to Scotland, and so had nothing to do with the tide of nationalistic feeling that had swept through both teams. Now, some months later, the two countries were to have another meeting and all hoped that this time things would go as they should.

The event was held at the Rushcliffe Leisure Centre in Notthingham and a large full crowd of friends and supporters gathered to watch the proceedings. In a small gymnasium just off the main hall both the English and the Scottish fighters had gathered to warm up and generally prepare themselves.

Suddenly the door to the gymnasium burst open and in came a rather hairy Scotsman. Until he appeared, all had been going smoothly as members of both teams exchanged mild and polite banter. Then the incoming Scot, clad in full national costume, kilt swinging, sporran gleaming, stomped around the room, singing a reble song at the top of his voice and stopping only to hurl insults at the nearest Englishman. To be quite honest I did not know what to think. At first it seemed rather funny but then his behaviour became more threatening and I could see that it was having a bad effect on the younger English lads who for fighting for the first time for their association. The incident also boosted the morale of the Scottish team. At last he was escorted from the gymnasium and to our surprise he emerged later as a member of the Scottish team.

The teams lined up and after the usual formalities the contests got under way. Things went at a pretty even pace and to the relief of all concerned there were no signs of untoward agression. Gradually the fighting got a little stronger and the inevitable accidents began. The first major incident came about half way through the first round. The English fighter was definitely the stronger of the two men involved and had for the most part taken the initiative. He repeatedly forced his opponent to the edge of the fighting area. Towards the end of the contest he made one more rushing attack. In a flurry of kicks and punches he drove his opponent yet again to the edge of the area and there delivered a series of kicks, one of which sank deep into the side of the Scotsman. He fell to the ground. The referee intervened and the fight was brought to a halt. It became clear that he had been badly hurt only after the two fighters had finished the contest and were sitting down. I remember vividly seeing the Scotsman kneel and then keel over, clearly in great pain. He was examined and an ambulance was sent for. I heard later that the unfortunate man had sustained a ruptured spleen, an injury which is

43

found in various other contact sports such as boxing and Thai boxing. The damage was no doubt caused by the kick which was seen to sink into his body.

The second accident happened some time later but this time it was an Englishman's turn to suffer. The man concerned came from Bradford in Yorkshire but I do not recall his name, even though I had seen him numerous times at training sessions and in competitions. He was fighting a Scotsman who seemed somewhat over agressive though neither man seemed to have the upper hand. Then, for what seemed no reason, the Englishman knelt down in the middle of the floor and held his left arm up. He was talking to the referee and although he tried to explain what was wrong he could hardly be heard above the noise of the excited crowd who were booing and cheering at the same time. Suddenly, as if by a pre-arranged signal, the whole room fell silent, and everyone saw the reason for the poor fellow's behaviour. What had happened was that one of his fingers had been pushed backwards from the knuckle joint and was now protruding through the skin in the palm of his hand! The skin of his finger looked like a concertina squashed back against the knuckle joint and the whole thing looked incredibly painful. He was rushed to hospital but the damage was done and I noticed years later that his hand was slightly deformed and would never return completely to normaility. As a concluding note to this little tale I might add that for my first fight that day I was drawn against none other than the Scotsman who had made his presence felt so raucously and insultingly in the gymnasium. Thankfully his bark was worse than his bite and I held him to a draw.

Chapter 5

It was about this time that I began to become a little independent of my instructor. This was not because I thought that I did not need him any more, far from it. It was something of a personal nature that began the eventual split between us. So before I tell more of my personal training in and study of Karate I would like to relate to you something of my relationship with my Karate instructor.

His name is Mr. David Vickers and when I began my training with him he was ranked Nidan or second degree of Black Belt. He ran his dojo with an air of fair minded discipline and dojo etiquette was strictly adhered to. At first I had very little contact with him, because the club's membership was so large in those days that a new student could go relatively unnoticed by the instructor. But as the months went by and as the people who had started with me began to drop out I started to come more and more under his direct supervision. Having said that, it took nearly two years before he began to take a direct interest in me.

Once he had begun to think of me as a serious student my training sessions became a mixture of pleasure and pain, and sometimes a case of sheer survival. Many times he pushed me to my limits, only to push me even further! At times I was convinced that he did not like me, and was waging some kind of personal vendetta against me. How stupid of me, you might say, but believe me sometimes even the other students thought

45

that I was on some personal hit list that the instructor had at the back of his mind. This belief was strengthened by the evidence that not all the students were treated in this way. It took me a long time to realise that I was one of the lucky ones.

One night after the lesson had finished I asked him if he would show me a Kata using Nunchaku, known in the media as 'rice flails.' He had always declined to teach me, saying that I had enough to think about learning how to use my hands and feet. This time, after I had been asking for months, he agreed to show me the Kata the following night. I remember going home and practicing until the early hours of the morning.

When the time came, I stood slightly to the side and behind my instructor. He told me to follow him step by step, slowly through the Kata. I ought to point out that this was a Kata of his own invention and not a traditional Okinawan form. We had gone through the Kata about ten times and it was beginning to stick in my mind when he said, 'One more time, and this time faster.' He did a combination of movements and I followed close behind. Half way through the Kata there is a technique where the nunchaku is swung in an arc diagonally across the front of the body and caught with the left hand on top of the right shoulder. As my instructor performed this move he looked to see if I had kept up with him. In doing so he missed catching the nunchaku and it hit him full in the mouth. I looked at him to see if he would carry on. He simply spat out a piece of broken tooth and did indeed carry on. He always had that controlled air about him and I often wondered what would happen if that controlled attitude were turned against someone.

By the time I got to know him better, things were beginning to go wrong in his private life. Without going into personal details it is sufficient to say that as a result his character began to alter. This was only apparent to people who had known him over a number of years. I knew that at times he was in great inner emotional turmoil but he never once let it affect his teaching of Karate. As I advanced through the various grades of Karate I became closer and closer to him and by the time I had been promoted to 2nd Kyu we had also become personal friends. I remember the first time he invited me to his home. It was like walking into a Japanese Aladdin's cave. Japanese swords hung on the walls, framed by the many certificates and diplomas which had been awarded to him during his years of studying Karate. He had a huge library of books on every conceivable martial art.

He had begun his training in the mid-sixties in the Wado-ryu style of Karate. In those days it was the best established style in the country. He never told me why he started training, but he did tell me something of those early days when toughness and spirit were the order of the day. No room then for theorising and building personal empires.

One could argue I suppose that the form of training which that generation received left nothing for personal development. But I believe that if you look at the Black Belts of today you see in the majority a marked decline in knowledge and skill. How many people do you know who, at the age of ten or even nine years old in the sixties, received their Black Belts? No, it took a special kind of person to stick with Karate in this days. Rough and ready they may have been but I believe that they were closer to the real spirit of Budo than many of the people involved in Karate today.

David Vickers' early gradings were with Mr. Tatsuo Suzuki, the Chief Instructor for Wado-ryu Karate. Later he was graded by Mr. Masafumi Shiomitsu who came to England to assist Mr. Suzuki. By the time he had reached 4th Kyu his instructor had decided to change his club's affiliation to the new style of Karate which was sweeping many parts of the

47

country – Shukokai. Within two years David took and passed his Shodan, Black Belt, grading. Just two years later he' was promoted to Nidan. He was always a good fighter and I learned a lot from his positive and confident attitude when in combat. I well remember everyone's faces when he turned up to fight on our first squad training session with the S.W.K.U.(E). Everyone thought that he was far too old to fight with all the tough young Karate-ka who were present, but I knew better. Needless to say he made the team and I felt very proud that we would be going to our first European Championship together.

I find it hard to put into words my feelings of gratitude and friendship for him. Towards the end of my time with him he did and said things which I did not agree with. However, I moved on as I believe all students should move on from their instructors – in friendship. For his help and guidance I shall be forever indebted and am indeed fortunate to have had such a good start in my Karate.

(Left to right) the author, Kenny Johnson, Jimmy Todd, in Charlesville, 1983, at the Shukokai's French Gassuku.

48

Chapter 6

In September 1978 I married. It was a small wedding with no fuss. This was in keeping with my newly developing attitude to life. My new wife Stephanie and I had saved hard for two years and had amassed sufficient funds to put down a deposit on a three year old semi-detached house. Shortly after we moved into our new home I received permission to open a dojo. I set about organising a club in the Reddish area of Stockport where we lived. Not being able to drive at that time limited me considerably but I did manage to find a location for a dojo and soon had a nucleus of sixteen students. On reflection I feel I may have been a little over zealous in my early days as an instructor. I can remember wanting everyone to be as enthusiastic as I was about Karate. I was annoyed and disappointed with people for not sharing my enthusiasm. I realise that in those days I was teaching for myself rather than for the students.

The following year I was asked if I would teach Karate at a local night school. I agreed to do so and this led to some of the most rewarding experiences I have had in my teaching career. When I walked into the large gym of the school where I was to teach I was amazed at the huge number of people who had turned up to learn Karate. They all wanted something, something which would make them tougher, or thinner, or stronger, or faster, or just something to make them feel less scared when they went out alone. I taught Karate at the night school for three years and learned during that time that Karate was all things to all people.

It was whilst I was engaged in teaching at the night school and at my own dojo that I received a letter. It was handed on to me by the secretary of the S.W.K.U.(E), Terry Murthwaite. The letter was from a man who, with others, had been practicing the Shukokai system of Karate for some months, but the Brown Belt instructor who had been teaching them had found running the club uneconomical and had simply informed them all that he had finished teaching. They wrote to Mr. Murthwaite and the letter was passed on to me. After a telephone conversation with the writer of the letter, Ian Standing, I agree to visit the club.

My first trip to the club was a seven mile, two bus journey and after a catalogue of lost connections and misdirections I arrived only three minutes late. Six students had turned up and as I listened to their story it became clear to me that their former Brown Belt instructor was none other than the man who had been thrown out of my first club back in 1974. He had turned out to be a real character and to show what I mean I will relate a tale involving him, my own instructor, and myself, to illustrate the extent of his deceit and treachery.

In the winter of 1977 I accompanied my instructor to witness a Black Belt grading. It was permitted in the association at that time for a 1st Kyu to witness such a grading, prior to taking it himself. Apart from the senior grades on the panel we had no idea who else would be there. You can imagine our surprise when we saw this man, lined up with the others; the man with the flair for letter writing. He had applied to the association with a cock and bull story about his family being about to emigrate to Australia, and about wanting to take the Black Belt grading before he went out there. The emigration ploy is not as uncommon as you might think by the way. As with most lies, things never seemed to be quite right and the panel, led by Mr. Bob Aikman, could not exactly see the relevance or importance of the emigration story as the Shukokai organisation is very big in Australia.

As he took his place I am not sure who was the more surprised, the letter writer or us. My instructor was on the grading panel and so asked for a private meeting of the members before the proceedings began. In it he explained how the Brown Belt with a love of writing fiction had featured in his life and also that he knew the man's family and none of them were setting a foot out of the district, let alone going to Australia! The panel took their places and the grading began. As part of the gradings in those days it was necessary for each candidate to declare his loyalty to the true spirit of Karate-do. I watched in eager expectation as Mr. Aikman asked the Brown Belt if he was of good character and not prone to lying or dishonesty. His answer was of course what he knew everyone wanted to hear but this was not enough. Mr. Aikman then asked him if he believed in loyalty to one's instructor. The answer came, 'Yes, Sensei.' Mr. Aikman continued, 'then why did you once fabricate a letter condemning your instructor?' He nearly choked. I watched his eyes darting across the room, backwards and forwards from David Vickers to Mr. Aikman. He stuttered and mumbled and no matter how he tried he could not come up with an answer to explain himself. He did not pass his grading that day, for, as Mr. Aikman pointed out, there should be more to a Black Belt than mere technique.

The fact that this same man, a few years later, should stop teaching people simply because they did not generate enough cash for him did not surprise me. What did surprise me though was the fact that he had not simply gone out, bought a black belt, and put it on anyway. Others have.

The new club began to falter soon after I began teaching there. For most, the contrast between their old instructor and

51

myself was just too much. Within six weeks the club was down to just one member. Ian Standing was the one whose letter for help had reached me but I don't think he envisaged himself turning up week after week for what amounted to private lessons. Slowly, people began to call at the club and ask for lessons and within a few months the dojo was echoing to the sound of 'Kiai's' and the number of students levelled out at fourteen.

That year the S.W.K.U.(E) had acquired the services of Mr. K. Tomiyama. Mr. Aikman had accepted the post of Chief instructor to Norway and so Mr. Tomiyama who was now married to an English woman moved to Leicester and began touring the association's dojos up and down the country. During this time I began to think of myself as a student of Mr. Tomiyama and less as a member of an association. This feeling of following the teaching of a man and not the directives of an executive committee has been with me ever since.

It was also about this time that I received an injury that almost changed my life forever. I had been on squad training in Nottingham and had, over the afternoon period, received three heavy kicks, two of which had hit my stomach. The other one was in the groin. By the time the session was over my body hurt. I drove the seventy odd miles back to Manchester and collapsed into bed. Though I have always had a high resistance to pain I was on this occasion fast approaching my limit. My wife ignored my protests and dislike of doctors and phoned for the emergency physician. He arrived after two hours with the words, 'What seems to be the matter?' I told him that I had been practicing Karate that day and had been kicked in the stomach and groin. He examined my abdomen and prodded it, and pushed it, saying, 'Well if you will do such a sport this is what you can expect.' He then told me that I was suffering from internal bruising, and left, having given me two pain killing tablets and the advice that I should get some sleep. The pills, like the doctor's advice, were useless and three hours later I asked my wife to phone for the doctor again. She did so and this time it took an hour for him to arrive. A different doctor came this time and after a similar cursory examination he came to the same conclusion and gave me a pain killing injection. By now I was totally confused but even so my body told me that there was something seriously wrong and yet two doctors had independently come to the conclusion that I was suffering from nothing more than bruising. The injection did its job and free of pain I fell into a deep sleep. I woke up about four hours later and felt the rush of pain, like a current of electricity shooting into my brain.

I tried to sit up but could not. I looked down and was horrified to see my stomach distended. It was positively bloated and my scrotum had swollen to twice its normal size. My wife phoned for an ambulance and I was rushed to hospital. There another doctor examined me and immediately summoned a surgeon. The look an his face was bordering on fury when I told him that I had been seen by two doctors. He took their names and the address of the surgery which they came from. I had been bleeding internally all this time and was in need of surgery. My testicles had been ruptured and there was some doubt about whether I would be able to keep them! There I was at the age of twenty-four and only married a year, in imminent danger of losing my manhood. The surgeon told me that he would not know what was to happen until he had operated and seen the damage. I woke next day finding myself full of tubes leading to redivac suction bottles to remove residue of the damage from me. The operation did not reveal that I would have to be emasculated and I recovered well. Ten days later I was released from hospital, happily in full possession of all my vital equipment.

My club was none the worse for wear after my absence because of the help from two very good friends of mine, Tommy Rowe and Steve O'Driscoll. They both hold Dan grades in Shotokan Karate and they had taken it in turns to teach at the club during my hospital stay. Over the years I have had many a happy hour practicing Karate with these two men and although our styles of Karate differ we know only that we love the art and our involvement with it. Whenever I visit Manchester I make sure that I have time to train with them for they are true Karate-ka and practice for love not money.

For some time I had had a student called Terry Harrison. What he lacked in physique he more than made up for in fighting spirit and determination. He also had the ability to organise; a quality which many people, including a lot of Karate instructors, do not possess. Having discovered this talent within himself he came to me with an idea for raising money for the club. This was especially welcome because the club funds rarely matched demands made upon them. From the beginning I had used any money which came in to pay for expenses incurred either by myself or the other students. Then came Terry's idea. For an initial outlay of £30.00 the club could, with the right permission, run a lottery and with the right kind of management might bring in as much as £70.00 per month. When things got rolling the club began to make so much money that we opened a club bank account. Among the many benefits that this brought were a club library, free trips and dojo equipment. Best of all it meant that we could receive a visit from Mr. Tomiyama every month without the worry of whether we would have sufficient funds to pay for him. On such occasions the training was free to the members. They had the best of the instruction without having to pay a penny. By this time I had consolidated my teaching and students at the Cheadle club and things were progressing nicely.

The Easter weekend of 1980 found me once again headed for the Continent. This time I travelled with Mr. Tomiyama and several others to the small French town of Charlesville-Mezerie. This was in the north eastern corner of the country. It was the occasion of the annual European course of the S.W.K.U. The course was directed by Yasuhiro Suzuki Sensei, 7th Dan, with the assistance of Messrs. Tomiyama, Omi, Okubo and Kamahara, all of whom were 5th Dan. This was also to be the scene of my Second Dan grading. Mr. Suzuki's method of instructing is always enjoyable. He never over-awes his students but pushes them on and on. This course was no exception. I recall how a year earlier when the course had been held in Belgium, Suzuki Sensei told us that we had been invited to a dance in the nearby village of Pepinster. Needless to say we all had a very good time out and next morning he asked us how we had fared; he knew only too well and started us off on one of the hardest training sessions I have ever had. By the time it was over, nobody was suffering from a hangover!

As the weekend progressed I began to get a little nervous. My grading was now only a day away, or so I thought. That afternoon the Black Belts were practicing Kata under the direction of Mr. Kamahara. Suddenly in the middle of the lesson Mr. Tomiyama called for the people who were attempting their gradings. This was it! I had no time to worry any more. There were five candidates including myself, although only two of us were attempting Nidan. Suzuki Sensei has a unique way of grading. He knows what he wants to see, and he knows how many mistakes he will allow you. As soon as you go over the allotted number of mistakes he will stop you then and there and end your grading. This may seem a little harsh at first but personally I feel it is better than the usual way of letting you go all the way through a grading only to be told at the end of it all that you have failed, because for instance of mistakes you made in your basics at the beginning.

We were lined up and numbered off from one to five; I was number five. The first part of the grading was Kata. All candidates were required to perform Kata from both Higaonna and Itosu groups and after we had all done two Kata each we were asked to sit. After some time and a lot of conversation between the Senseis Suzuki and Tomiyama we stood up to hear the outcome of their exchanges. Mr. Tomiyama then began to tell each one in turn that Mr. Suzuki felt that more time was needed before they could be graded up to their next level. He then asked them to go back to their lesson. This left me, the lone survivor of the first section of the grading. I stood there wondering what would come next. Mr. Tomiyama then asked me what was my favourite Kata. I told him that it was Shiho-koso-kun. 'Then please do it,' he said.

A mixture of confidence and nervousness filled my performance of this Kata yet I did it to the best of my ability under the circumstances. The two Sensei discussed my performance in Japanese. It was like waiting to see if I were to be executed. What could be next was the question which ran through my brain. The conversation stopped and Mr. Tomiyama asked me to stand sideways on to Mr. Suzuki. I felt that I was under the miscroscope and imagined all sorts of things going wrong with my Karate. Having thus completed various techniques using both the left and right sides of the body I was allowed to sit down and rest whilst Mr. Tomiyama went off to find an opponent for me to fight. He returned with a rather well built Frenchman whose name I did not know. We were destined to become friends and I learned that he was called Andrea Beurtlhoff. He was a student of Mr. Omi's. I was not looking forward to this contest as I had seen Andrea fight before. He had represented French Shukokai for many years and to be quite honest I felt that he was in a higher class as a fighter. However I had no choice.

Within seconds of the fight starting Andrea slammed in a very strong front kick which sent me reeling back across the floor. This was just what I had expected. I had visions of being thrown around the hall. Panic began to add to confusion and both emotions joined forces to consume me. Mr. Tomiyama called stop and returned us to the starting line. Off we went again. Another front kick sent me staggering back but this time I responded immediately. I blocked his second kick and countered with a string of punches followed by kicking and punching combinations. Once again Mr. Tomiyama called us to a halt and as we took our places once more it crossed my mind that it was only at me that Mr. Suzuki was really looking and only me who was being marked for techniques and spirit. When the combat resumed I set about Andrea like a man possessed. I have no illusions about the outcome of the fight had it been for real but as it was I gave a good account of myself. That was the important thing. After four or five minutes we finally stopped. Andrea was dismissed to his class and I was left alone. After some further discussion between the Senseis Mr. Tomiyama turned to me to deliver my doom. 'Mr. Clarke,' he announced formally, 'Mr. Suzuki says that you are now Nidan.' As I collected my new licence from Suzuki Sensei he stood up and shook my hand, at the same time telling me to go back to my class. I bit of an anticlimax may be but I was on cloud nine. This was in stark contrast to what awaited me at home.

My return to England was not what I had imagined it would be. For some time I had been heavily engaged in Karate. I had been running my own dojo, the night school class and a class I had been asked to run for the Boy Scouts' Association. On top of this I was also having discussions with a boy's boarding school about setting up Karate lessons for their pupils. In all this time I had been neglectful of my marriage; not purposely so but neglectful all the same. If only I could have foreseen the emotional upset which was coming. My wife had always been very proud of me and my involvement in Karate but she found it very difficult to come to terms with what she saw as my addiction to it. She was nothing more nor less than a Karate widow. My welcome home was like the gathering clouds of a marital storm to come.

That summer Mr. Tani arrived with a team of instructors from Japan. To train under Tani Hanshi had long been an ambition of mine and I was full of excitement at the prospect of its fulfilment. Never did I dream that I would be formally presented to him as one of the senior instructors for the association in England. To crown this I was presented with a small gift from him as well. Training with the actual founder of a fighting system is quite an experience. Watching him perform techniques, I could see Tani-Ha-Shito-Ryu done at its purest. He moved with a smoothness and agility that belied his advanced years and I enjoyed his instruction enormously. Unlike some Japanese I found him approachable and willing to answer my questions even though his command of English was not so good.

It was easy to see why so many people had been attracted to this style when when it was introduced to England in the late 1960's. In Japan also the new Shukokai must have swept over the Karate world like an autumn wind. Although the forty-eight Kata studied in the Shukokai are drawn mainly from the Higaonna and Itosu groups the style has a look and feel like no other. The revolutionary concepts of the double hip twist, kick shot, zero, snap, shoulder shock and many more makes this a unique form of Karate indeed.

At this point I feel I should explain the difference between Shukokai and Tani-Ha-Shito-Ryu. Mr. Tani began his training in Karate with the founder of Goju-ryu, Master

Miyagi. Later on he changed his studies to Shito-ryu under its founder Master Mabuni. He went on to become a personal student of Master Mabuni's and in time was presented with a master's diploma by him. In 1948 while Mr. Tani was working as a teacher he opened his own school of Karate and called it the Shukokai, which means 'an organisation where people of progressive thinking within Karate can come together for mutual study and development of ideas.' However, the style of Karate practiced at the Shukokai is Tani-Ha-Shito-Ryu, which means Mr. Tani's sect of the Shito-ryu school of Karate. In Japan there are other sects of Shito-ryu Karate such as Hayashi-Ha-Shito-Ryu and Abe-Ha-Shito-Ryu, the Masters of which sects were both given Master certificates by Master Mabuni.

The weekend course flew by, and soon I was left with just wonderful memories. Boosted by my experience of training with Mr. Tani and the other Japanese instructors I returned to my dojo with renewed vigour. At about this time I rather stupidly developed a dislike for Karate competitions. I say stupidly because my feelings grew to ridiculous proportions and blinded me to the need for small but important parts of one's overall training. Also I was stupid because I allowed my feelings to come between Mr. Tomiyama and myself. Fighting had always seemed important to me but I had begun to dislike more and more the sporty razamataz which surrounded competitions. The continuous bickering between officials and team managers was very distasteful, as was the bantam-cock strutting of some of the better known competitors. All in all I felt that this was far removed from the original concept of Karate contests. Most of all it was the downright dishonesty that pervaded the whole of modern day Karate competition that finally made me turn my back on it.

Things came to a head at the S.W.K.U.(E) annual general meeting. After it I still had the impression that the association was spending far too much time and effort on competition related activities. Soon after that meeting I wrote a letter of resignation to the S.W.K.U.(E). I wrote too to Mr. Tomiyama explaining the reasons for my actions. Although I must plead guilty to being strong minded and even stubborn I have always been sincere in my actions. I did not at the time plan to join another association as I did not want to change the style of Karate practiced at my dojo.

Mr. Tomiyama being the man he is answered my letter. He explained his own philosophy and also pointed out some truths about me. I would like to say that there are things about all of us that from time to time should be aired. However this is not an easy thing to do but even so I feel it should be done. By then I had started travelling with my friends from Shotokan, Tommy and Steve, to Liverpool. Once a week we would train at the dojo of Mr. Terry O'Neill Sensei who was to leave a lasting impression on me. His method of instruction was first class, always talking and giving advice, encouraging and pushing. He works very hard when instructing and never stops till the final bow. I am sure that anyone fortunate enough to have trained with him will always be the wiser for it. The mere forty minutes of travel to reach his dojo was small in price for the knowledge gained.

I used to travel to Liverpool every Wednesday night and on one such occasion I returned to find the house empty. It was 11.0. p.m. Where was my wife, Stephanie? I still do not understand why, but I began to get angry. Where could she be at this time of night? Why no note of explanation? The phone rang. 'Hello,' I said. Stephanie's voice answered. 'Mike, it's Stephanie here.' I noticed that her voice was trembling. 'I've got something to tell you.' I never gave her the chance to go any further. 'Listen, anything you have to say to me you can say at home, don't go running off like some bloody teen-ager.' By now I was shouting! 'Mike, my mum's been found dead.' Her voice broke down and she began to cry. I was speechless. It took me a few seconds to realise the gravity of the words I had just heard. This was the depth to which I had sunk. Involved in my Karate, like a drug addict living only for his next fix, oblivious to all but my own interest, Stephanie was all but excluded from my awareness. I drove round to her parents' house. I tried to console her as best I could but however I tried I felt overwhelmingly inadequate.

Author vigorously attacking with a front kick.

61

Group photograph taken after the author - extreme right -
first met Tani Sensei

Higaonna Sensei, Liverpool, 1982. The author is on the right,
and John Boyle, 2nd dan, on the left. John Boyle introduced
the author to Goju-ryu Karate.

Chapter 7

It took me almost a year to realise the wisdom and the truth contained in the words Mr. Tomiyama had written to me after my resignation from the Shukokai. I needed an instructor of my own. Training with O'Neill Sensei was wonderful but after the death of my wife's mother I travelled less and less to Liverpool and as I wanted to continue practicing Tani-Ha-Shito-Ryu I could think of no one in England better to learn from than Mr. Tomiyama. After long discussions with a friend and after much thought by myself I decided to ask Mr. Tomiyama if he would accept me back as a student. As I have said before, I had seen myself more as a student of Tomiyama Sensei and less as a member of an organisation. So it was that I felt I had to ask him first if he would teach me again and if he agree then I would apply once more for membership of the S.W.K.U.(E).

I used the occasion of the 1981 Shukokai European Championships to meet Mr. Tomiyama. The Championships were to be held at the Meadowbank Stadium, Edinburgh and I remember feeling extremely nervous as I made the long drive up to Scotland. The event was made special by the presence of Mr. Tani, who, with a small party of Japanese instructors, was in Scotland as part of their European and Scandinavian tour. On seeing me my old friends gathered around to find out how I was, and how my Karate was going on. It was good to be back in their company and I felt warmed by their friendship and genuine intent.

The time had come for me to seek Mr. Tomiyama and do what I had come to Scotland to do. I saw him first from the other side of the large sports hall, and as I walked towards him I felt as though all eyes were on me. The walk seemed to last forever. As I came near him he turned towards me and looked straight at me. What would be his reaction to my request? I bowed and we exchanged greetings. 'Sensei,' I said, 'I have come here to ask you if you will allow me to become a student of yours again.' His reply was immediate. 'Yes, everything is forgotten.' As we shook hands he said, 'Go and see about joining the association again.' I bowed and went to find the secretary of the association.

The following Easter, I was once again in Charleville-Mezerie, in France. The course that year was directed by Senseis Omi, Okubo and Tomiyama. I had travelled with Mr. Tomiyama to the course and because of a hold up we arrived much later than planned. Tomiyama had a room reserved for him but I had the last one available. On this particular course I did not have a grading looming in front of me and so I enjoyed it all the more. When I went back home I was full of new ideas. My students have always gained from my travels, since it has always been my opinion that techniques should not be withheld from students unless it is in the interests of their safety. But two weeks after I returned from France I was taken seriously ill. My temperature rose alarmingly and I was stricken with diarrhoea. The doctor came and with a mixture of sarcasm and roughness he examined me. I was sent to the local hospital and once there I was put in isolation. Doctors came and went, asking me questions and examining me once again. Then a plastic valve was fitted to a large vein on the back of my hand and numerous samples of blood were taken. Huge doses of antibiotics and anti-coagulants were pushed into me. I was weaker by the hour. Then I was asked if there was anyone I would specially like to see; things were not looking good. But fate was not ready for me yet and as I slowly recovered I asked the doctor what was wrong with me. He smiled that smile that doctors learn in medical school and said, 'I suppose I can tell you now, you had had Legionnaires disease. But don't worry you are getting better.' Stephanie was with me at the time and we just looked at each other in silence. Neither of us had realised how close to death I had been. I was annoyed with the doctors for not telling me. Later on the doctor told me that in his opinion I had survived because my body was so fit from all the training I had done. As far as I know there is no cure for this dreadful disease and the plain truth is that if your body is not fit and strong you will die from it.

My convalescence seemed to take for ever and to this day my lung capacity is not what it once was. During this time my students were training under the same two friends who had come to the rescue before, Tommy Row and Steve O'Driscoll. At this time my Karate settled into a period of quiet progression. I had even less interest in association matters but I did support the association when it became necessary. My main aims were to further my understanding of Karate, not just technically but the theory and the history. I wanted too to grasp the larger picture of the art and not just that within the association. I had begun to build up a library of books and video tapes. But my main help came from conversations with Mr. Tomiyama. He told me the history that he knew and the chief differences between some of the main systems.

During such talks, he would often challenge me to look inwards at myself and examine my own faults and attitudes, unravelling the prejudices I had towards people and things of the Karate world. I learned to become less naive about the politics and to keep my views to myself if the situation required it. In the past I had always been ready to air my views no matter who was hurt. Tomiyama Sensei taught me to go beyond my own annoyance at things and look further than outbursts of verbal vengeance, finding the cause and probable solution to my problems. He said that impetuous behaviour would slow down my progress in Karate; my mind would be hindered by my seeking retribution on the offenders against my own personal code of conduct. He was right. Karate should be a method of building one's character in a positive way, and Tomiyama Sensei showed wisdom and patience in teaching me this valuable lesson. In the years I spent as his student I don't think that I learned anything more fundamental and true than that. I have been fortunate in having good instructors and I always remember him for acquiring the possibility of thinking things through before expressing an opinion.

In August of that same year, he returned to Japan for an indefinite period and I felt alone without a Sensei. My ties with the association were not very strong ones and so did nothing to alleviate this feeling. During the summer months a friend of mine, John Boyle, who practiced Okinawan Goju-ryu Karate, told me that Morio Higaonna, 7th Dan, was coming to Liverpool. Higaonna Sensei is the chief instructor for the world in that style and his visit to Liverpool for a weekend course was open to all styles. Steve O'Driscoll and I decided that we would go and train under him. I was amazed at the strength and mobility of this new teacher. I had seen high ranking instructors before but never anyone to match the control of the body displayed by Higaonna Sensei. I was immensely impressed by his Karate. It lacked some of the more dynamic postures of Japanese karate but seemed a very practical system. I felt very much at home with the techniques, even though some of them were new to me. The first day of training concentrated on basic techniques, especially hand techniques but also introduced me to a Goju practice known as 'ude-kitae' or arm pounding. This consists of two students striking one another's arms and wrists together in various ways. This is painful, at first, but after some time it becomes bearable, just! The second day was spent working with a partner and I remember enjoying myself a great deal with this new system; new to me that is. I drove home on the Sunday evening filled with exhilaration. Higaonna Sensei's impression on me had been strong, technically and also as a man. He had been approachable by all, showed a good sense of humour and was thoroughly liked by everyone.

In September of that year my wife Stephanie and I decided to divorce. It had become obvious to both of us that our interests and more importantly our aims in life were far removed from one another. However, if it is at all possible to have a divorce with a happy ending then we at least achieved that much together. She and I are still great friends, seeing each other occasionally and both having new partners with whom we are very happy. The ordeal of divorce though, however amicable, is a great emotional drain which leaves one physically exhausted too. Only by constantly recalling my conversations with Tomiyama Sensei did I find the strength to go forward. At times it seemed that only my Karate held me together. Some might say that it had been Karate which had brought me to divorce in the first place! In an effort to get away from my problems I left England for America. I have relatives in the U.S.A. and by going there I hoped to find some kind of distraction. But before long I realised that the answer lay not across the Atlantic in a new country but within myself. I soon returned to Manchester and began to rebuild my life.

Sparring with Vickers Sensei.

Dave Vickers Sensei, 3rd dan, the author's first instructor in Karate, in the Japanese gardens of Tatten Park, Knutsford, Cheshire, 1979.

Chapter 8

The Chief Instructor for the S.W.K.U. (Channel Islands) is Mr. David Moss, 4th Dan. I had met him first four years earlier on a European course in Pepinster, Belgium. Over the years we met repeatedly and I had spoken to him before I left for America. He knew all about my situation and invited me over to Jersey. I arrived in March 1983 and thanks to the marvellous hospitality I received from David, his wife Vanessa, his students and friends I settled into Jersey life quickly. My training under David began shortly after my arrival and also I met once more my friend Andre Bertlehoff from Paris. He had come to Jersey on holiday and to visit friends, for he had once lived on the island himself. I recalled my sparring with him during my Nidan grading three years earlier. We had met several times since then. The Jersey Shukokai dojo is housed above the Jersey weight training centre in St. Helier, the capital. When I saw it for the first time I knew that I would enjoy my time there. It was a refreshing change to be a student once again. I enjoy instructing but always prefer to be a student. My first lesson consisted of timing and speed training both with and without partners. David Moss is very fast and his thin build gives no hint of his strength; he is capable of delivering very heavy blows. This is due to his mastery of bodyweight distribution. In his early years as a Karate student he had been a top class competition fighter and amongst his many honours was Great

69

Britain All Styles Brown Belt Champion, Shukokai Black Belt European Champion and finalist in the Shukokai World Championships held in Japan in 1976. Unlike a large number of successful competition fighters David had learned his art thoroughly and after his competition days were over he had made the transition to Instructor easily and with great success.

I accompanied my new instructor to France that summer. This was to be my third and last visit to Charlesville-Mezerie. Also, it would be my last European course with the Shukokai. David and I flew to Paris where Andre had arranged to meet us. This was my first visit to Paris and I liked the city very much, with its broad streets and tree-lined boulevards. It reminded me a little of Copenhagen and was in complete contrast to New York where I had been earlier in the year. In fact when we arrived we were met not by Andre but by Kenny Johnson. Kenny is from Nottingham and we had become friends from the time I joined the S.W.K.U.(E) in 1976. We had trained together many times and taken part in competitions as representatives of Shukokai in England and abroad. It was not long before we were joined by Andre and amidst crazy jokes and laughter we got into his car. Driving in typical crazy French fashion Andre delivered us to our destination in record time. The course was directed by Senseis Omi and Okubo. The course once more boosted the system and gave an opportunity to make new friends and renew old friendships.

A few weeks after my return from France I met Kathy Penney. She had come to Jersey to visit a friend of hers who was working at the hospital in St. Helier. Our first meeting was not a great success but fate had decreed that we should cross paths again, which we did; the next afternoon!

It was my custom during the long Jersey summer to join a friend, Terry James, for tea at a favourite beachside restaurant of ours every Sunday afternoon. It was on one such afternoon while he and I sipped our tea and quietly solved the problems of the world that I had my second encounter with Kathy and her friend. They joined us and Kathy ended up drinking most of my tea. After a somewhat limited conversation she helped herself to my buttered scones too. We arranged to meet again that night when I promised to treat her to the delights of Jersey night life in the shape of the Channel Islands Aero Club. For my part I thought the night was very enjoyable. Kathy had a good sense of humour and was bright and intelligent. What is more she possessed better than average good looks. She did not smoke and she drank pints. I remember commenting to a friend that she was almost perfect – for a woman that is! We set up another date the following Wednesday night after my Karate training. I had planned to take her to Corbier Point to see one of the wonderful sunsets from there. But fate once more showed its hand.

On the Wednesday afternoon I was asked by my Instructor if I would teach the lesson at the dojo that evening as he would not be able to get there on time. I was more than happy to do this for him but now I had to make a slight change to my original plans. Because I would be in charge that night I would be responsible for locking up. This made it impossible for me to make a quick getaway and thus make it to Corbier on time. I contacted Kathy and asked if she would mind coming to the dojo. She welcomed the idea and said she was looking forward to seeing Karate at first hand. When she arrived I told her to sit at the back of the dojo. This was a beginners' class and so nothing exciting was happening. But after an hour I called the class to a halt whilst I explained to the students the importance of injecting rhythm and expression into their kata. Suddenly, one of the students on the back row threw himself violently to the floor. I recognised his actions immediately for what they were – epilepsy. I had dealt with epileptics before and knew how to assist them

71

during a fit. However, this man had struck the floor very hard with his face as he fell and now a considerable amount of blood was coming from his mouth and nose. I was worried in case he might choke on his blood and so was more than glad when Kathy took over. As a State Registered Nurse she was much better qualified than I to deal with the situation. She kept his airways clear and despite the blood soaking into her clothes she continued to assist him until the ambulance arrived. He was taken to hospital and after a few days he recovered.

Over the next two weeks of Kathy's holiday we spent many hours together and as her holiday drew to a close she decided to give up her place in a teacher training college and move to Jersey. She flew home and arrived back ten days later. Since then we have been inseparable.

My Karate improved considerably that year, thanks to the instruction of Dave Moss and in November 1983 I accompanied him to Nottingham for a weekend course organised by the English S.W.K.U. Sensei Omi and Sensei Okubo took the course and Sensei Tomiyama had come from Japan. I had decided to try for the next grade which was Sandan – 3rd Dan. As I took my place in the line-up for the course to begin I knew that it would be a strenuous one. On the first day we completed three two hour sessions and I for one was exhausted. The second day was only a little less demanding, with two sessions. During the course there was a meeting of the Shukokai European Committee. Students had come from Sweden, Norway and France, as well as from Scotland and different parts of England. Then there was our party from the Channel Islands.

For some time since Mr. Suzuki's return to Japan in 1981, the Shukokai World Karate Union, Europe, had been thinking of changing the name of their organisation. There were many reasons for this change of name, not the least of which was

72

the growing number of groups using the word Shukokai as part of their title. The new name for the organisation was the Kofu-Kan. This was still a mainly Shito-ryu based system, however the Goju aspect of Mr. Tani's Shukokai was brought into more prominence. Also, since the Japanest instructors in Europe had decided to follow directly Mr. Suzuki as opposed to Mr. Tani it was felt more honest to have a name not belonging to Mr. Tani. Henceforth the organisation would be known as Kofu-Kan Shito-Ryu-Do Karate. The Honbu Dojo (Central Dojo) of the system is in Tayota City Japan, where Mr. Suzuki now lives and works. Mr. Tani recognises Mr. Suzuki's deviation from his Shukokai and has endorsed his move.

The course came to an end I sat down happy but tired, to await my grading. Two others besides myself lined up for the test. The method used for the grading was the same as that used by Mr. Suzuki. In the Kata section I decided that I would do a long and intricate Itosu style Kata called Kosokun-Dai. I did this because Itosu style Kata had always been my weakest and I wanted to show my examiners that I could in fact perform my weakest Karate to a good standard. My second kata was Seieanchin. Here I came across an old problem. I had followed the teaching of my instructor on Jersey diligently, but the interpretation of the kata as practiced on Jersey differed from that required by the examiners. The three Japanese Sensei discussed my performance and then announced that I had performed the kata wrongly. I can't remember why I picked Tensho for my last kata but I do recall thinking how badly I had done it. I had not done it for a long time and although I knew the physical moves I had little or no feeling for it. Therefore my kata was weak and I was justifiably criticised for it. My fate was sealed; I did not get past the kata stage of the exam and in fact no one else was successful on that day.

73

I don't want to try to find unreasonable excuses for my failure on that day but I would like to voice an opinion in print. I feel that the changes which are often made in kata by various members of a group can only lead to confusion. It is impossible for every member of a group to keep in touch with every change in a kata. I also think that if a student displays an understanding of a technique and can execute it with speed, power and correct posture then that student should be deemed knowledgeable in that technique. Therefore, just because a student performs an 'old fashioned' move in a kata it should not go against him if he performs it according to the above criteria. At the same time I acknowledge the right of my superiors to organise training and grading just as they see fit.

Shortly after our return to Jersey I discussed with Kathy the possibility of going to Japan. We were thinking of returning to live in England and it seemed to me that if we wanted to go to Japan then this would be an opportune time to do so. Kathy had never been abroad before and the prospect of travelling to the other side of the world on her first trip was a little daunting. I assured her that she would be all right and that she would enjoy her trip to the far east.

After much thought and conversation with my instructor I decided that we would go to the Island of Okinawa. If possible I would find Mr. Higaonna of the Goju-ryu and ask if I could train with him. We left for Okinawa on February 2nd 1984.

Chapter 9

We arrived in Naha on the third at 7.30 p.m. after a.journey of over thirty hours. We were both very tired and looking forward to a good night's sleep. It was cool and wet as we stepped from the plane, on to the coach and thence to the airport buildings. I should point out that at this time Kathy was under the impression that I had an address or phone number through which I might contact someone. But I had not been successful in obtaining either before we left. She knew that I did not know Mr. Higaonna's address, though I only told her that when we were on the second leg of our journey, high above India!

I had hoped that we could complete the formalities of entry fairly quickly, but as anyone who knows the Japanese will be aware they do not rush anything, least of all something official. We were the last people through the passport control and therefore last at the customs. It was here that something happened that I believe could only happen in the east. The customs officer we were approaching was very scrupulous. We had watched him searching the luggage of other passengers with horror. He was not only checking the handbags of the women but even their purses and lipsticks. When we reached his bench the customs hall was all but empty. I had already undone all our locks and zips but when we reached him he stood and looked at us. Then in broken English he said, 'Where you come from?' Kathy replied, 'England.' A broad smile began to crease his face. 'How long you stay in Okinawa?' 'At least a month,' I answered. 'This is long time for vacation; why you come to Okinawa?' 'I have come to train with Sensei Higaonna of the Goju-ryu.' 'Ah, so, Karate!' He went on. 'Higaonna Sensei very strong.' He continued, saying that he did Karate himself as a young man, and then asked me to show him my knuckles. He was a little disappointed when he saw that they did not bear the large callouses he had expected. These usually accompany Karate training in Okinawa. 'How long you train in Karate?' 'Ten years in Shito-ryu, not Goju-ryu.' That seemed to do the trick. He bowed to us both and waved us through, wishing us a happy stay. We walked through the swing doors that led to the front of the building. 'You know something, Kathy,' I said, 'he never even glanced at our luggage!'

I was to discover during my stay in Okinawa, more than once, how my practice of Karate elevated me in the eyes of the average Okinawan. This is because they see Karate training as a serious undertaking, and not just a hobby. The fact that I had done it for ten years was to an Okinawan a testimony to my character. We took a taxi into Naha and on the way I asked the driver to take us to a European style hotel. He took us to the Hotel Ekka, one of the top hotels in Okinawa. We knew that this would be expensive but we did not cherish the thought of spending our first night sleeping on the floor. By the time we had checked in and reached our room it was 9.30 p.m. It was then that I told Kathy that I did not have a single contact. She just laughed; she was too tired to worry.

Still tired but filled with eagerness, I rose early on Saturday morning. It was vital that I find Mr. Higaonna that day, for staying at the hotel Ekka would leave us with no funds in a very short time. I went at first to the tourist information desk in the front of the hotel. There I obtained a map of the city. Then I went to the check in desk and asked the clerk if he would look in the telephone directory for me and find the number of a Mr. Morio Higaonna, and his dojo number. He soon found the dojo number, but as Okinawan directories only list the number and district and not the full address I gave the map of the city to the clerk and asked him to circle the district where the dojo was. His pen traced the area on the map, and he told me the name of the district was Makishi. This was a little over two miles from the hotel. I felt much better in myself then and decided to go for a short walk and take my first proper look at Okinawa.

It was about nine in the morning and people were hurrying to and fro along the streets. School children swelled the throng, on their way to school and every now and then one of them would wave to me and shout a greeting in English before scurrying off in fits of embarrassed laughter. Usually it was, 'Hey, Joe' or 'Peace, Man,' or some other American phrase. As there were many American military personnel there we were always assumed to be Americans too. People were always surprised when they found that Kathy and I were English.

On the way back to the hotel I witnessed something uniquely Japanese. As I passed a used car lot I saw the salesmen, mechanics and office staff jogging around the cars. After three or four circuits of the cars they stopped and formed a large circle. Their appointed leader then took them through a series of exercises which, as I stood and watched, impressed me by their similarity to the exercises we use to warm up in Karate. I tried to imagine English or other European people doing this kind of thing at work. I decided that the Japanese, who have an almost fanatical wish to belong to a group, are unique. They have a special nature, peculiar to themselves alone.

Kathy was still sleeping soundly when I returned to the hotel. But time was short as we had to vacate our room by ten o'clock that morning and with nowhere to sleep we had to arrange lodgings, and hopefully the start to my Karate training!

The hotel staff had taken a keen interest in our search for Mr. Higaonna and as we checked out they insisted on minding our heavy bags until we had found somewhere to stay. They had also acquired a taxi for us and informed the driver of our destination. After a short drive through the busy streets the driver pulled to the side of the road. 'Makishi, Makishi!' he called as he pulled the lever to open the rear passenger door.

Before I continue with the events of that first day in Okinawa I would like to tell you a little about Japanese taxi drivers. First of all they are a clan and a law unto themselves. The way they drive their cabs is reminiscent of the fighter pilots of World War Two. Overtaking from either side is quite acceptable and all journeys are done at top speed. In all the taxis I used the drivers always joined in with the conversation going on in the back of the cab, sometimes at the expense of their driving. Near misses are counted in every hundred yards and one soon becomes quite blase about it. Although I must say in their defence that in all the time I was there I never saw a single crash. There is a saying in Naha that the population of people is one million and the population of cars is two million. I am not sure if the figures are accurate but it is true to say that the volume of traffic is so high that it seems like rush hour all day long.

We stood on the pavement and watched the taxi speed away at break neck pace only to squeal to a halt fifty yards along to pick up another fare. It was now up to us to find our way from the main street to the Karate dojo of Higaonna Sensei. After ten minutes of walking through the maze of back streets that make up the district we came across a small bicycle shop and decided to go in and ask for directions.

'Ohayo, gozaimasu,' I said, bidding the shopkeeper good-morning, in my best Japanese. As he did not speak English I went on as best I could. 'Tetsudatte kudasai masu ka. Karate dojo no Higaonna Sensei wa doko desu ka?' He smiled and answered me but his speech was so fast that I could not fully follow what he was saying. However he did convey that the dojo was not far away and after making sure that we knew the way he confirmed that it was the right dojo by pointing to his little finger and thumb and asking if the man I was looking for had a wife who was a foreigner. 'Gaijin,' he said. 'Hi, yes, gaijin.' I should explain that in days gone by the little finger and thumb were used to depict a man and woman. The older generation still use this symbol. I thanked the shopkeeper for his kindness and patience and bade him 'sayonara'.

Sure enough, within minutes of following the directions we had been given we found ourselves standing outside the dojo we sought. To be honest I felt a little apprehensive standing there, at the place we had come half way round the world to find. I could hear some movement from within, and hesitantly knocked. The door began to slide open, focussing my thoughts on how we would explain our presence at the dojo. In the doorway stood Terauchi Kazio Sensei. I bowed and asked if Sensei Higaonna was inside. 'No inside,' he replied in his rather rough voice. 'You come back at four o'clock.' And he slid the door closed.

Kathy and I looked at each other. What now, I thought; we could not afford to wait around all day until four, so I decided to call at Mr. Higaonna's home, which is above the dojo. Again I knocked on a door, wondering what our reception would be. This time it was Mr. Higaonna's mother who came. I bowed and asked if he was at home. Her reply was too quick for me to follow but she smiled and beckoned us inside. We stepped into the small area reserved in all Japanese homes for the removal of footwear, and having put on some house slippers we were invited into the living room. We were

79

made to feel at home and given tea, biscuits, cake and sweets. I explained who we were and what we were doing in Okinawa. Mrs. Higaonna said that she was happy that we had come so far to train with her son. After about fifteen minutes she excused herself and made a phone call. She spoke for a while and then called me over to the phone too. I did not know what to expect and hoped it would be Sensei Higaonna; it wasn't, it was his wife, Alanna. As I said earlier, she is not Japanese but American, from Los Angeles. It was refreshing to hear English spoken again and I was able to explain exactly what we were doing there and what we hoped to do. Alanna thought we were 'nuts' to do what we had done, and said she was also amazed that we had found the dojo. She explained later that even Japanese visitors from the mainland got lost trying to find it. I asked her if she thought that Sensei Higaonna would allow me to train with him. She said that he was there and that she had explained our presence to him. He would be only too happy for me to practice at his dojo. Alanna asked me where we were staying, and then told us of an inexpensive Japanese style hotel that visiting students usually use. She added that Sensei Higaonna would be coming to the dojo in half an hour and would personally take us to the hotel. We waited for him in the empty room which Sensei Terauchi had now vacated.

We sat, talking in whispers until finally the door slid open and in stepped Sensei Higaonna. He gave us one of his broad smiles, exuding happiness, and immediately we felt relaxed and at ease. I introduced Kathy and myself and formally asked for permission to train at the dojo. He agreed and said he was delighted that I had gone to so much trouble to train with him. As we walked through the narrow streets to the hotel he asked me about England and about my training. We deviated a little from our route to call at Alanna's aerobics studio. She also has a wonderfully open and friendly personality, making us feel welcome and at home in a manner which can only be achieved in one's own language. We also met Sagi, their son, who looks just like his father, possessing as well the same bubbling sense of humour which runs right through the family, combined with a seemingly endless spring of energy resources.

We left the studio and continued to the hotel, which lay beyond a small fruit and vegetable market. Sensei introduced us to the owner, Mrs. Sumiko Kinjo, whose establishment was known as Minshuku. Sensei was a little worried that we would not be comfortable sleeping on tatami mats but I assured him that we would, and in fact that we had hoped for just such a room. It was typically Japanese, the size of seven tatami. It had a small alcove in one corner. There was almost no furniture; a small table in the centre of the room being the only item. Sensei said that he would negotiate a price for the room, as low as possible! This was typical of how Higaonna Sensei looked after us during our stay, making many things easier for us. As he was leaving he told us that training began at 7.30. am. the next day, Sunday.

When he had left we took a taxi back to the hotel Ekka. The hotel staff were delighted that we had found Higaonna Sensei and good lodgings. As we drove away again with our luggage the staff bowed and waved to us until we were out of sight. We both needed some more sleep, as it was late in the evening. We took a shower, I dug my Karate gi out and left it ready for the morning. Then we collapsed into sleep.

81

(Left to right) Virra, Mr. Kobuta, Sensei, Michael Ch'ing
and author, Okinawa, 1984.

(Left to right) Tin Nee Ch'ing (wife of Michael Ch'ing),
Kathy Clarke with Seigi Higaonna on her knee, an aerobic
instructor of Alanna's, Alanna Higaonna, the author, Virra,
Higaonna Sensei, Christina Larsen.

Chapter 10

I will always remember that first Sunday morning. I left
Minshuku at 7.0. a.m. and as I walked through the bustling
market the enormity of my actions suddenly hit me. Here I
was in Okinawa where it had all begun. What would happen
if the other students took a dislike to me? How would I cope
with the Goju style of Karate? My mind recalled stories of
foreign students being beaten over and over again to test their
spirit. Would this be my fate? I trudged towards my first
Karate lesson in the land of its birth.

On arrival at the dojo I found that I was one of only
three students training that morning. The senior student was
Terauchi Kazeo, 5th Dan, whom I had met briefly the day
before. He is a native of Tokyo, but often spends long periods
of time on Okinawa training under Higaonna Sensei. He is
extremely strong and has an unnerving appearance. In spite
of this in the weeks to come he proved to be a very helpful
instructor and spent a lot of time explaining to me the finer
points of Goju-ryu.

The second student was like myself, a Gaijin or foreigner.
His name was Vildrsidarem but thankfully he was known as
Virra, for short. He is a native of Penang in Malaysia and
had come to attempt his Shodan or first Black Belt grading.
He was living in the dojo. The weather was warm and heavy
and I began to think that I might have difficulty training in
such humidity. Sensei arrived and my previous nervousness

vanished. We began a warm up routine that was to precede every session of training from then on. After twenty minutes of this we put on our training shoes and left the dojo to begin jogging.

We set off at an easy pace down the hill and on to the main street of Makishi and within a minute we reached the local park. We ran round the perimeter of the park; I lost count of how many times, and cursed myself for not having kept up my running back home. By the time we left the park to run back to the dojo the weather was as hot as the warmest summer's day in England. I was feeling the strain.

At the end of every run, Sensei lines his students up at the bottom of the hill that leads to the dojo. From there it's a fast sprint up the hill, finishing at the sliding doors of the dojo. I was determined to be there first, and after a mad dash, I was, just. Terauchi-san was not pleased. Once inside we began to go through more exercises but this time of a more strenuous nature than the earlier ones we had done. They consisted of weight training and stamina exercises, interspersed with plenty of push-ups, squats and sit-ups.

It was after such a repetition of seventy-five sit-ups that I began to feel sick. I quickly asked Sensei to be excused and rushed to the toilet at the back of the dojo. There my stomach began to expel its contents – nothing. Only digestive juices came out for Kathy and I had eaten nothing since our arrival in Okinawa two days earlier. What with all the excitement we had simply forgotten to do so. Sensei Higaonna was quite concerned about me and sat by me at the open doorway giving me warm water to sip.

As I sat there watching Terauchi-san and Virra practice their Kata under Sensei's watchful eye I became embarrassed. This soon turned into anger against myself for not being able to control my body and not continue with my first lesson. When the lesson was over I apologised to Sensei Higaonna for my lack of stamina and told him I was ashamed about the whole thing.

He told me not to feel that way and said that there is no disgrace in pushing oneself and in fact finding one's limit, whatever those limits might be. However if one holds back for the sake of comfort then that is a shameful thing to do, and then one should feel ashamed. I saw the truth of this and realised how stupid we in the west can be when it comes to dealing with questions such as this.

The lesson over I wended my way back to Minshuku, slowly, hoping that the warm weather would not last, for this was supposed to be the Okinawan winter. As I went past the little bicycle shop where the owner had been so helpful the previous day, he bowed to me and shouted his greetings of good morning, as did his wife and family who hurried out from the back of the shop. I thought what a wonderful place this was. Then I quickened my pace as my thoughts turned at last towards the subject of food.

Kathy was still fast asleep when I returned, but soon woke up and confessed also to being ravenous. After a shower we set out to explore the city and find somewhere to eat. Naha is unlike any European city I have visited. Like other Japanese cities it has no street plan clearly recognisable to me. I can best describe it as being like a giant maze. However at no time did I feel uneasy or concerned as to which part of the city I might find myself in. In common with other Japanese cities, Naha has little or no street crime as we in England know it. Therefore this fear is removed and one can walk freely.

Sunday is like any other day, for the Japanese are not Christian, except for a very small minority. As a born Christian myself I witnessed more practical Christian behaviour in Okinawa than I have ever seen anywhere else. Apart from a few exceptions the Okinawans are a kind, considerate and friendly people. They take great pleasure in the simple things of life and cherish the family system. Every house more or less has a colour television set and music centre but they still marvel at the simple, natural things of life. Houses old and new are besieged with plants, trees and shrubs. During our time there, people always could spare some of their time for us and showed great patience towards us as foreigners in a strange country. I wonder how a visitor to England would fare in the streets of London without a command of the English language. I concluded that the qualities needed to be a good Christian are the same as those needed to be a good Hindu, Jew, Moslem or Buddhist. Are they not also the same qualities needed to perfect our characters and behaviour through the constant practice of Karate-do. Surely that is the 'do' we all profess to follow is it not?

After a short time of walking through the narrow little streets we suddenly came into a broad, bustling thoroughfare called Kokusai-Dori or International Street. It got its name from the many foreign items on sale in it after World War Two, and it is the main shopping centre of Naha. At each end there are two large Okinawan Lion-Dog statues. Through the years, Kokusai-Dori has kept pace with the western world and as a result seems a little out of place in the context of the rest of the city. Kathy and I found it a gift from the gods for along with all the foreign goods was also foreign food! This meant, for us, food from home.

The first familiar name we saw was 'MacDonalds', and as we walked through the doors towards the hamburgers we were greeted by a sea of bowing heads. The small army of young attendants were eager to please, especially as they assumed that we were Americans. There was some discussion between them as to who should try out his English first on us and then the oldest looking stepped forward and said with a perfect American accent, 'Hi, can I help you sir?' We gave him our order of four egg muffins and six portions of French fries, a large tub of coke and two teas.

'Right away, sir,' came the prompt reply. We did not have to wait long for the food either and when it did arrive we set about it with vigour. Once finished we rejoined the bustling crowd in the streets and returned for a good night's sleep.

Monday morning and I was up early once again, but this time feeling much better. I walked slowly to the dojo, sure that I would finish the lesson this time. The bright humid weather had been replaced by cloud, and the wind, that seems to be always present in Okinawa, was blowing even more strongly. My first lesson that day began with studying various aspects of Karate kata. Sensei Higaonna taught me to take a kata and work at it from different angles. For instance sometimes he would have me work at a kata fast, sometimes slow, sometimes strongly and then softly. In other cases he put the emphasis on stances, then again on hand movements. All in all it was a very informative lesson for me and one that stands out as the most enjoyable. The second lesson was at 7.30 p.m. and it was here that I met the majority of the students for the first time. To my surprise one of the students was a visiting Nidan from New Zealand, Christina Larsen. She had originally come to Okinawa for a six week trip and had ended up staying for a year. From the first we became friends. I was impressed by her ability to be a very strong Karate-Ka and at the same time remain very feminine. My training began to pick up from that day on, and my attitude underwent a change. It was as if I began to see Karate in a different light. I saw things about training I had never previously thought of. Also I was attracted to the realistic approach to Karate that the Okinawans have. I felt that the kata were less symbolic of combat and more closely related to reality. I already knew most of the thirteen kata used by Higaonna Sensei because Master Tani had begun his Karate with Bushi Miyagi, the

87

founder of Goju-ryu and had kept some of his kata in the syllabus of the Shukokai. However, Master Tani did change them a little to suit his own ideas. I soon picked up the changes in technique although the change in the feeling of the kata was a bit more difficult to obtain. My training schedule was from 7.30 a.m. to 9.0. a.m. and 7.30. p.m. to 9.30 p.m. on Monday, Wednesday and Friday and there was a 7.30 a.m. lesson every Sunday. I was early to discover that although lessons began on time they rarely if ever ended on time, as often Sensei would teach through to 10.00. p.m. and sometimes to 11.0. p.m. Though I was glad of the extra training I was often glad when he called the class to a halt.

On that first Wednesday I was introduced to traditional Okinawan weight training. As well as the weights there are too some traditional training aids. The various tools and devices fall into two categories: those which you strike and those which you grip. There is one exception to this description which is the kongoken which is designed to be wrestled with. Perhaps the best known aid of all is the makiwara which takes its name from the type of straw which is wrapped around it, or rather round a post set firmly into the ground. The post and the straw together are called makiwara. The Karate student strikes the straw until it is finally torn away and then a new bundle replaces it. Most modern makiwara have leather padded targets instead of straw ones which makes life less messy and increases the life span of the aid. This device is used to promote correct posture, balance and focus.

There are also less well known striking devices which are posts known as Udekita, and To, as well as the makiwara. Since gripping plays a major part in Okinawan Karate there are devices for promoting the grip. Though all the training aids used today were originally found in use in daily life on the island and adapted for use in Karate training, they have largely been replaced by manufactured items, especially designed for Karate students.

My personal favourite training aids were the chi-ishi or strength stones and the gami or jars. I took to training with these two very quickly and often practiced with them on my own in between lessons. Not so with the makiwara . . .

I had seen makiwara before in England and even tried punching one from time to time, but I think, like most people in the British Isles, I had thought that they were used for developing large knuckles. But on Okinawa I found what a useful device the makiwara is once you know how to make use of it. As I said before it can develop your stance, balance and focus. Knuckle 'development' is a mere side effect which comes from continuous punching and focus.

When I remember Friday nights in Naha I think of exhaustion. After that first Friday night's training I was more exhausted than I have ever been in my entire life. It began like any other training night. I had arrived early and was spending time going over the kata which I knew. It was at such times as this that I received a lot of help from some of the other Dan grades. Terauchi-san and Yonisato-san were particularly kind to me in this respect. Between them they would watch my technique and point out where I was going wrong. Terauchi-san focussed on the kata and Yonisato-san on the applications of the kata. Within the Goju-ryu system an organised method of application is taught known as bunki. This involves training in pairs and has the effect of bringing the kata even more to life than when one trains alone. Once again my earlier training in Tani-Ha-Shito-Ryu was of great help to me, for that system also uses practice drills taken from kata known as Hokei-Kumite. Although they are not quite as complex as those done in Goju-ryu they give very similar benefits if done thoroughly.

That Friday evening it was drawing close to 7.30 p.m. and

89

the dojo was filling up with more and more students. People were coming from other dojo in Naha, as was their wont at the end of the week. They did this for a number of reasons, but most of the young Black Belts who came did so for one reason – to fight. Sensei arrived and the lesson was soon in progress with exercises followed by the practice of basic strikes, punches, blocks, and kicks, in static and moving phases. After an hour like this, everyone was fully warmed up and ready for the next section. We paired off to do ippon-kumite, and after twenty minutes we were called to a halt. Only the Dan grades do free fighting at Sensei Higaonna's dojo and so all the Kyu grades were told to sit at the back and observe. Although contact to the face is frowned on, the body is expected to, and does, receive, heavy blows. This is done without malice and the students know what to expect.

All was going well until I found myself facing a student from Uehara Sensei's dojo. His name was Yamashiro. He fought as if his life depended upon it and within seconds he had kicked me several times on my upper legs in an effort to slow down my counter attacks. I suspect he was also trying to demoralise me from the outset. He forced me back the full length of the dojo and his kicks all the while became stronger. It was obvious that his confidence was increasing. As I crashed against the wall he kicked again and this time I knew that he meant to really hurt me. From that moment my own attitude changed completely and I launched into an attack that sent him in turn reeling backwards. My final combination ended in an ashi-barai or ankle/leg sweep which sent him to the floor with a resounding crash. He sprang to his feet like a cat. I knew that I had to prove to him, and to everyone else, that I could not be taken lightly in combat. As soon as he was on his feet I used ashi-barai again and followed it immediately with a mawashi-geri or roundhouse kick to the stomach. He fell down on to one knee, holding his arms tightly round his body. To be honest I had never kicked anyone as hard as that before, and I was quite surprised how effective my left foot could be. After that our practice together was a little more restrained and sensible, but I knew that he would try again. When the training was over Yonisato-san told me that I had done well. On Friday evenings, he pointed out, the visiting students always tried to beat Sensei Higaonna's students. It is done in a friendly atmosphere and obviously the visitors had considered me to be fair game. By stopping Yamashiro-san so decisively I had demonstrated to them that I was no pushover. This event made me feel very relaxed in the dojo and I felt that I was increasing in confidence and mental and physical strength.

The following Monday morning Sensei Higaonna decided to take me sight seeing. I was not exactly sure what he meant but I welcomed it as a change. The other students did not share my confidence and had I known what was in store for me I would not have felt the way that I did either. The sight seeing tour is in fact a run and it usually ends at Shuri castle. This monument, which is now in the process of being re-built, stands high on a hill above the city of Naha and the hill itself seems to stretch upwards into infinity. The route we took to the top was via an old cobbled roadway that was laid down at the same time as the castle itself was built, in the fifteenth century. It was used mainly by tradesmen. In places the gradient is one in three and as Christina said as we struggled to the top, 'It's good for your soul!'

When we reached the castle Sensei Higaonna gave us a short tour of the grounds and pointed out the places of interest. He also showed us where Higaonna Kanryo Sensei used to go running. After that it was back to the dojo, but this time it was all downhill and the running was much more relaxed. The rest of the morning's training was in kata.

On Wednesday night the lesson was taken by Terauchi

91

Sensei, as Sensei Higaonna had gone to the airport to meet Virra's instructor from Malaysia. His name is Michael Ch'ing and he had come to Okinawa for two weeks of training and also to attempt his Yondan grading. He and his wife were due to stay at the same hotel as Kathy and I, and so we all got to know one another very well over the next two weeks.

Friday night came around once again as it always does; I found myself wondering if Yamashiro-san would also turn up again, and if he did, would he adopt his aggressive attitude again. He did, and this time I was determined to be the more positive if we should meet. Sure enough we did partner up for Ippon Kumite, or one step sparring. As expected he tried very hard to land his punches on me, but as I had anticipated this it was easy to block his almost desperate attacks. His frustration at not being able to actually hit me became evident in the next part of the lesson, Jiyu Kumite or free fighting. Yamashiro-san had as his partner not me, but a young shodan of about eighteen or nineteen years of age and this poor lad bore the brunt of his anger. This did not go unnoticed by Sensei Higaonna and I knew that Yamashiro's time would come.

The class was called to a halt, and a quick glance at the clock revealed that it was almost 9.30. 'Ah,' I thought,' a few cooling down exercises then it's back to the hotel for a shower and then sleep.' But as anyone who knows Sensei Higaonna will tell you, when he is in a good mood he is in the habit of forgetting the time and so instead of cooling off a very tired class he sent us on to do arm pounding exercises. Just as my arms were about to fall off he called out, 'Yame', or stop. This must be the end, I thought to myself, but no . . . The class was told to sit at the back of the dojo and from there Sensei called them out one at a time. He had put a large leather pad on his arm and with this he moved around the dojo positioning the pad in different ways, calling out one technique after

92

another. You were obliged to execute that named technique as quickly as possible and as hard as possible. As you can imagine, your physical limits are soon reached with this kind of training. It is then that Sensei Higaonna starts to move faster and call for the more difficult techniques. He takes you past the point where you would usually stop and makes you work until you can work no more. I must admit that this kind of training hurts, but afterwards I was overwhelmed by my sense of achivement. I felt that I had progressed and made new ground where I had previously failed. Such ability to draw the maximum from a student is the mark of the true Sensei, and remember that all Black Belts are not Sensei.

The clock was showing eleven when we lined up and the lesson came to an end. I walked back to the hotel thinking that Friday night was definitely not a night for the fainthearted.

Since my return from Okinawa I have been asked more than once if I was allowed to wear my black belt, as if my belt colour gave me some kind of power of knowledge. To be quite honest I felt somewhat embarrassed about having to answer. This was because the question was always asked by someone who was wearing a black belt, and I found it hard to believe that they lacked sufficient understanding to refrain from asking it. Before I tell you the answer to this silly question I would like to tell you of an event that took place one evening in Okinawa. It was a Friday night, with visiting Black Belts as I described earlier. As people readied themselves for the training to come the door slid back, with five minutes to go to 7.30 p.m., and in stepped a young man whom nobody seemed to know. He spoke to some of the senior grades and was then shown to the changing area. He emerged from behind the curtain and, as I expected, he was wearing a black belt. I thought nothing more of it but I recall that it caused quite a stir among the other students.

In Sensei Higaonna's dojo as in all other dojos it is the

senior students who line up in the front row and the lower grades behind. The lower your grade the further back you stand. In this dojo there are always two or three rows of Black Belts at the front and the unknown visitor took up a position in the second row. All was as usual as the class started and we went through the very thorough warming up period. It was only when we had moved on to the practice of Kihon-waza, basic technique, that the stranger began to stand out as someone unusual. This was because he was having difficulty in understanding and performing the required techniques. This difficulty became more and more apparent as we went on, and it was obvious that he was not up to a standard expected for Dan grade, and certainly not in this dojo. When we moved on to Ippon Kumite and Jiyu Kumite, free fighting, it was here that the stranger was punished for his presumption in wearing a black belt. It is understood that gruelling hard work is needed to gain black belt, and I got the distinct impression that the other students felt insulted by the stran-ger's indifference to their endeavour. So much so that he got an extremely rough time with the other Dan grades and he was left in no doubt about how they felt about him.

At first I felt a little sorry for him for he had indeed been put through the mill but on reflection I now feel it was right for them to chastise him. I argued with myself that if this testing of people were not done then anyone could stand with the seniors and this detracted from the efforts that the junior grades were making to reach a higher standard. Although I had not realised it I had gone through the same scrutiny and testing myself during the first week of training and had even so maintained my place at the end of the row, the front row.

And so the answer to the question about wearing my black belt in Okinawa is a brief 'yes'. But in fairness I should say a little more about it than that. First of all I fully realise how hard it is for a Kyu grade student to understand me when I say that having a black belt around your waist means very little. Of course it is good to know that you are getting somewhere with your training and being awarded your black belt shows that you are at least mastering the basics. But over the years I have seen so many people wearing black belts who have such a small understanding of Karate that I place little value on it. It is indeed sad that today people are awarded black belts for being good at competitions or worse, as political favours.

I believe that the belt should indicate the wearer's knowledge and understanding as indeed it used to. It should be an outward sign of the struggle within and the progress one has made. The Okinawan students I practiced with had no great interest in grades; they were much more interested in gaining knowledge and mastery of the techniques, and this they did with great effort and determination. Sensei Higaonna himself only graded at the insistence of his superiors and the fact that he was awarded third dan stands as a testimony to the length of time he had trained without a grading. Those among us today who would have people believe that they are more than they are have only my pity for they have missed the true meaning and secrets of Karate-do.

Sensei Higaonna using tonfa at Michael Ch'ing's home, 1985.

Sensei Higaonna performing 'Saifa' kata during a visit to Michael Ch'ing's home in Penang, Malaysia, January 1985.

Chapter 11

Life on Okinawa was not all blood and thunder and the following Sunday a group of students, including Kathy and myself were invited to Higaonna Sensei's home for dinner, Sensei used to live above the Dojo however he now lives about half a mile away. The house is of traditional Japanese design but inside it has all the benefits of a modern western home, including a very modern kitchen which Alanna had made use of and provided us all with a marvellous meal. For me it was a great personal honour to be asked into his home. During the day we sat around eating, drinking, and talking about many things. It's on occasions like this that I felt the warmth and caring character of Higaonna Sensei, for I truly believe him to be a Sensei of the old school. That is to say he genuinely cares for his students and that they in turn care for him and look to him for advice and leadership; in fact one could say he is almost a father to his students, as were the Sensei of old.

Before we left Sensei presented Michael Ch'ing, Virra, and myself with a copy of his latest book, in each he had written a personal message making each book a treasure to the proud owner.

Monday morning soon came and once again I found myself pounding the streets of Naha. I should like to point out at this time that Sensei does not run very fast but he does run for a long time, and at the same speed irrespective of the many hills in and around Naha. After an hour's running we returned to the dojo for more kata practice. I found the practice of kata early in the morning to be very beneficial. The Monday night's lesson passed by without incident and afterwards Sensei invited a few students to join him the next day for a trip to a bathhouse, Japanese style. We were to train first for one hour then visit the baths. The following morning I joined the three other students at the dojo and shortly after Sensei's arrival we began our morning's training. The lesson was to consist of makiwara practice for the four of us, and by the end of the hour my knuckles were cut and bleeding quite badly. However I was determined not to stop unless Sensei said so. During everyone's time at the makiwara Sensei gave instruction and encouragement, stopping only to correct stances or change hands. My everlasting impression from that lesson was of how fierce an opponent the makiwara is. After our training was over we all set of to find something to eat and from there to the bathhouse.

For those who are interested in this particular form of Japanese relaxation I will relate to you my experiences on my first visit. First of all I should explain that bathhouses are used to relax and enjoy oneself in, and not to wash. When you have removed your clothes you take a shower or a walk through bath. Once clean there is a large variety of baths for you to enjoy; the bathhouse I visited had eight different types. These included a sauna, steam room, jacuzzi, whirlpool, and a cold bath. There was also an other type of bath that I particularly enjoyed, this involved sitting waist deep in warm water while a heavy wall of water falls down on top of you from a large pipe above your head. It's hard to describe the feeling but I suppose you can imagine that it's like sitting under a waterfall; it's very refreshing and as I said it was my favourite of all the different baths. After you have enjoyed your bathing there is usually a room set aside to relax further while you watch T.V. and have a cold drink. Finally there is a dressing room fully equipped with mirrors, hair dryers, brushes, and even after shave. In fact everything you might need to make yourself presentable to the outside world.

The following Friday was the day Michael Ch'ing and Virra had been working for; it was the day they would attempt their gradings. The morning's lesson was given over exclusively to the practice of kata. Higaonna Sensei took us through basic and advanced forms; I had practiced all but the kata 'Shi sochin' before. This kata was entirely new to me; although I had heard the name I had never witnessed it before. Sensei preformed the kata for me and in it I saw the subtle strength that permeates Goju-Ryu. Sensei had me repeat it many times and soon I could remember the strange pattern, however it would take many long hours of practice before I could perform the kata with any degree of skill.

The evening lesson came all too soon for my friends Michael and Virra, and I could see the nervousness building as the lesson began. After an hour of fairly rigorous training the class came to a halt and we were all asked to sit at the back of the dojo. Higaonna Sensei sat down behind a small table that had been placed at one end of the dojo and after a little preparation he called Virra's name. A very nervous Virra took up position in the middle of the floor and prepared to start his grading exam with his rendition of the Goju-Ryu kata.

The first kata would be 'Sanchin' which is the fundamental kata of Goju-Ryu, at the same time it is also the most advanced as it contains the essence of the Goju-Ryu. After what was in my humble opinion a very good performance of Sanchin Virra was then asked to demonstrate the kata 'Gekisai-dai-ichi, Gekisai-dai-ni, and finally 'Shi-Sochin'. From there Virra moved on to the combat side of his grading. First 'Ippon-kumite' or one attack prearranged fighting, then 'Jiyu-kumite' or full freestyle fighting. Virra fought with most of the other brown belts present in the dojo that night, and also with two of the black belts. After this exhausting section of his grading he moved on to the final test, that of supplementary training. On this occasion Virra had to demonstrate his punching power on the Makiwara. The grading was now over for Virra who bowed to Higaonna Sensei and thanked him for his time in grading him.

For Michael it was the same thing, with the addition of the kata 'Saifa' and 'Sanseiru'. However as Michael was attmepting his Yondan grading he would also have much more fighting to do than Virra. When this part of Michael's grading came almost all the black belts present, including myself, were called out to fight him. During his third fight Michael injured his knee and it was obvious he was in pain; Sensei stopped the fight and examined his leg. He told him to rest for a moment.

Higaonna Sensei then called Yonisato-san to the center of the dojo. I was not aware of what was going on at first but when Yamashiro was then called out things did begin to dawn on me. This was to be Yamashiro's come-uppance. As soon as Higaonna Sensei had shouted to begin Yonisato leapt at his opponent and began a deluge of kicks and punches. Time and time again Yamashiro was knocked to the ground, standing only to be knocked down again. The fight lasted only ten minutes or so, but I should imagine Yamashiro thought it would never end.

Everyone knew this was a lesson in self control. For just as Yamashiro had been ruthless with the young shodan the week before he had now experienced the other side of that encounter. If he is intelligent, and he is, he would not let his emotions get the better of him again.

Michael continued with his grading, however the damage done to his knee was causing him concern and from then on his fighting ability began to diminish. He finished his grading like Virra, facing the makiwara, where I might add he proved to have a very strong punch.

With the gradings over the whole class lined up and the evening activities were brought to a close. When everyone had changed Higaonna Sensei announced the results. Michael Ch'ing had not been successful in his attempt at Yondan, however Virra had and was therefore promoted to Shodan. He was justifiably delighted.

That weekend Kathy and I along with six others accompanied Higaonna Sensei and Alanna on a sight seeing tour to the north of the island. We stayed overnight in a small town next to the ocean and Sunday morning found most of us following Sensei on a run through the town and on to the beach which ran for three miles along the coast. We ran the length of the beach and afterwards facing the sea we followed Sensei through the kata Sanchin. Later that night we finished the weekend off with a visit to an American restaurant; Yonisato thought it was amusing that Kathy and I should be so excited at the prospect of eating steak, and even more amused that we had it with boiled potatoes.

The weekend had been a great success with everyone enjoying each other's company, and on leaving the restaurant Sensei said that although he would be at the dojo as usual the next morning it would be o.k. for us to take the morning off and have a rest as he knew how tired we all must be. It's true we were all very tired; we had driven well over a hundred miles on the bumpy roads of Okinawa, we had had late nights and early mornings. However we were all present at the dojo the following morning and all though Sensei didn't say so I suspect he was pleased to see us.

On Monday night Michael Ch'ing, Virra, and myself joined Terauchi-san on a visit to the dojo of Kina Seiko Sensei 10th Dan. His dojo was small even by Okinawan standards, however Goju-Ryu does not require a large amount of space and so the size was more than adequate. Kina Sensei is the oldest remaining student of Miyagi Chojun Bushi still training and teaching every day. I was introduced to him by Terauchi-san who is a friend of the family.

After training had finished Kina Sensei handed out cups of hot Japanese tea and we all sat down to listen to this remarkable man. Kina Sensei does not speak English and does in fact speak in the old Okinawan dialect, however he makes himself understood easily by his actions. I could only sit and listen and be in awe of this man, for he is living history. For almost an hour we sat and listened to Sensei's comments and views on karate and life. He said he was very pleased to see I had come to Okinawa to study Goju-Ryu and even had his son demonstrate kata from both Shorin-Ryu and Shorei-Ryu while he explained the fundamental differences. His enthusiasm for karate was infectious and I felt honoured to be in his presence.

The next day I said farewell to Michael Ch'ing; we had got on really well over the two weeks he had been on Okinawa and before he left he invited Kathy and I to visit him and his family in Penang; an invite we hope to take up one day. At the end of that week we also said goodbye to Christina and Virra who were also returning home after extensive training on Okinawa.

Higaonna Sensei told me that he too would be leaving Okinawa soon to visit his students in India, and so with Sensei leaving, Kathy and I decided to make plans to return to England. We had vowed to stay on Okinawa as long as we could however with no jobs we had to depend on the savings we had brought with us. Kathy had estimated that our savings would last for approximately three weeks allowing for two good meals a day, our hotel bill, and my training fee, also a small amount was set aside to buy souvenirs. We had hoped to find some kind of work but unfortunately we were unlucky.

As this was possibly the one and only time I would get to Okinawa, Kathy and I took another look at our finances, and after some drastic cuts we found we could prolong our stay by a couple of weeks. The new budget by which we lived left enough money for just one small meal a day and absolutely no extras at all. We reserved our seats on the next possible flight home after Sensei's departure, however Kathy and I were now existing on 500 yen a day and on the day we left we had just 16 yen between us.

On my last morning's training session with Higaonna Sensei the class trained with the traditional training aids. It was while training with one such aid that I strained an old injury of mine in my groin; the pain was immense and so I stopped training in the hope it would subside in time for the evening's lesson. Unfortunately it did not subside and I was forced to watch the lesson from the back of the dojo. Kathy had come to the dojo to say her goodbyes to Sensei and to thank him for all he had done for us during our stay. I joined her in thanks to Higaonna Sensei for my training and for his instruction and patience. He apologised for not having done more for us and said he felt he had done very little. We were quite taken aback by Sensei's statements for both he and his wife Alanna had treated us like old friends, indeed the hospitality shown to us by everyone was overwhelming. Sensei then presented us with a small gift each. We said our final goodbyes and Kathy and I returned to Minshuku.

I have over the years met many high graded teachers of Karate both English and Japanese. Not all were from the same system as the one I studied but then I have always tried to look beyond my own style to see what there was to learn from a different approach, and I am always intrigued to see how different styles solve the same problems. However although the Karate side of the instructors was nearly always impressive I found their personal conduct almost always fell

103

short of what I had come to expect from such high ranking Karate-ka.

I do not feel I am in a position to pass comment on the behaviour or moral standing of such people; suffice it to say, things do go on that should not. I should like to make it clear though that this is not always the case, but next time you are on a weekend or summer course, study the behaviour of the senior grades. If they are not behaving courteously at all times, or if they have a fondness for drink and women then you must ask yourself whether they have the right to chastise you in the dojo for being weak spirited or lazy.

In all my time then, I have met few who are what they profess to be. One of the few people I have found to be all that other people profess him to be, and I say other people because he is much too modest to profess to anything himself is Morio Higaonna Sensei of the Okinawa Goju-ryu.

Lesser people may think him outside the dojo to be a little slow, quiet and even reserved, but this is because he is always at great pains not to put himself or anyone else in his company in a bad light, and so, ever vigilant, he elects to remain silent and let others do the talking.

There is a saying in the East that a true master will often appear to be simple. This saying can I believe be applied to Higaonna Sensei, though maybe the word simple is not the best one to use in translation. However it is true that Higaonna Sensei will always be the most courteous person in your company, he will always be the one to hold open a door so that others may pass through. I remember on one occasion in Okinawa where, had I not been on my guard, I might well have put myself before my Sensei and although he would not have held it against me I would have carried the feeling of disappointment with me for ever after.

It was towards the end of my stay on Okinawa and one of the many friends I had made was also about to leave for home. It was Christina Larsen and she was returning home to New Zealand after a rather long stay. To mark her departure several of us including Higaonna Sensei visited a small traditional restaurant close by the dojo. We were shown to an upstairs room and after settling down our orders were taken. After a time the owner of the restaurant appeared with the first meals and it so happened that they were for Kathy and myself. The food was placed in front of us and as the owner left she asked us all to forgive her for being so slow but explained that the restaurant was particularly busy and she would endeavour to serve us all as quickly as possible. The food on our plates was steaming and the smell drew everyone's attention to Kathy and me. Higaonna Sensei asked me to please begin eating and for a second I almost did, however thankfully I had the presence of mind to realise the position I was in and tapping Kathy with my foot under the table I told Sensei that we would be happy to wait until he and everyone else had been served also.

At first Sensei just nodded and carried on talking to the other people around the table, then when it became obvious that the rest of the food would take some time to arrive he once again asked us to start our meal. Again I declined but Sensei said that our food would get cold and that we should not wait for the rest; I did however decline to start although I did so in as polite a way as I could think of. We were to be asked once more before the rest of the food actually arrived and as before Kathy and I said we would be happy to wait. When the rest of the food did come the meal Kathy and I had ordered was almost cold but we mentioned nothing of this to our companions. I will always remember Sensei looking over to Kathy and me, and saying thankyou, he bowed. Although Kathy was a little confused about the whole thing I explained to her later that I felt we could not eat before Sensei Higaonna as this would be showing discourtesy and although he had told us to eat I could still not bring myself to do so.

To show further what I mean about the nature of Higaonna Sensei I will relate to you one more tale. This story was first told to me on one of the many visits to Alanna's dance studio that Kathy and I made during our stay on Okinawa. I asked Alanna if Sensei could drive a car and I was surprised to hear her say no. I then asked why that was so as I felt that most men of Sensei's age could drive.

Alanna then began to tell me a story that left me feeling that this was the stuff legends were made of.

Some time ago Sensei and a group of students had hired bicycles and gone for a trip along the beautiful coast. Okinawa is to Japan what the Channel Isles are to Britain and in the summer the whole island is teeming with holiday makers. This makes traffic even more congested than it usually is. As you might imagine cyclists in this kind of traffic have to be ever on the lookout for the many madcap drivers that live on Okinawa, as indeed they do everywhere.

Now Sensei being the man he is never goes for long without thinking of Karate and it seems that the fact he was riding a bike along a road made no difference. Of course he does not drift off on purpose, it's just that to Sensei Karate is his life and as such his mind is forever exploring it.

However it was unfortunate for Sensei that at this time while he was riding his bike and thinking of Karate he collided with a car. No one was hurt, however the owner of the car was furious, for you see it was a new car and obviously his pride and joy. He leapt from the car and shouting threats of violence he was determined to strike Higaonna Sensei. Fortunately for him he was stopped from doing so by the other students present. There then followed a terrible row with the driver of the car demanding satisfaction and the students desperately trying to calm the situation and explaining to the driver the impossibility of the task he was contemplating.

Sensei bearing witness to the whole thing was deeply moved that he could, through his own carelessness, have aroused so much emotion and anger in someone, and returning home he vowed never to ride a bike or drive a car or indeed allow himself to bring out such rage in another human being again.

What you make of this tale is up to you, I know it to be true because I was told it by Alanna. As I have said before a real master will often appear to be soft. Other lesser 'Masters' would no doubt have allowed the driver to attack him and then endorsed their own superiority by beating him senseless in front of the students.

On our last weekend Alanna took Kathy and me on a last sight seeing tour. We drove into the centre of the island and high into the mountains that run through Okinawa like a backbone. We visited the remains of a huge castle that was once the home of the kings of Okinawa. The day was warm and sunny and Alanna was a perfect guide. That evening Alanna presented Kathy and I with yet another gift; this was a personal present from Higaonna Sensei and Alanna to us. It is hard to describe how we were feeling at that time but I think humble is as close as I can get.

We left Okinawa on the following Tuesday, suffering slightly from the effects of our Seionara party. Alanna had taken us to the airport and before she left she echoed the words we had heard many times the night before, 'Please come back soon'.

The flight back to England was long and tiring but eventually we found ourselves landing at Heathrow Airport.

With the landing came the beginning of our new struggle to make a living in England once again.

Sensei Higaonna taking things easy at home with son Seigi,
Michael Ch'ing and author.

Sensei Higaonna at Quimper, France, 1986, with author.

Chapter 12

I have over the years heard many people speak of styles within Karate, usually in the context of one style being superior to another. Of course the better style the person is talking of is almost always the one he or she is practicing. It is a pity that some people who have been involved in Karate for along time still see things in this way. I remember reading some years ago that according to an old Okinawan Karate master there are no such things as styles within Karate, only emphasis. I also remember thinking – quite foolishly – how wrong this person was. It was only years later and after much more serious study of Karate that I came to the same conclusion as that Okinawan Karate master.

For those of you who do not study Karate I would like to explain as best I can what I see as the apparent differences that exist between one form of Karate and another.

Well, to pinch a word from an Okinawan Karate master, emphasis on technique is the main thing that distinguishes one style from another. Perhaps the best, or clearest, example of emphasis of a Karate type combat system is that of Tae Kwon Do. This Korean fighting art may look to the public like any other type of Karate. But in fact it has taken a significant step to the side of the main stream of Karate, in that the emphasis within Tae Kwon Do is on Kicking ability. Now anyone who has trained in Karate for longer than a few months should know that the term 'Karate' translates to

English as 'Empty Hand'. As you might imagine from this description of a fighting system the main weapons of attack and defence for a Karate practitioner would be his hands. Kicks do have a place in the Karate-ka's arsenal, but very much as a secondary ability after the hands. However in the Tae Kwon Do this principle has been reversed, and kicking ability has been given greater emphasis than punching.

So why the shift in emphasis from punching to kicking? Well for as many people as there are training in combat systems, there are as many opinions on how things should be done. The fact that the Tae Kwon Do have shifted their emphasis to kicking is quite irrelevant; there is room for such a move in emphasis because Tae Kwon Do as a system works, and that I believe is the criteria for what is and is not acceptable. As long as people don't go overboard with their opinions people can and do live quite happily together. However there are those who use this very kind of reasoning to hide their own inadequacies by excusing themselves for bad or unworkable techniques with statements such as 'Oh, this is how we do things in our style'. How many times I have heard this from the mouths of so called Karate Black Belts. The truth is that any person who holds a Black Belt in Karate should be capable of training with others of a different style with the minimum of difficulty.

If you do not yet practice Karate but are thinking of starting then may I be so bold as to offer you some advice. Take your time. Have a look around at as many people as you can first, and come to your own opinion as to the ability of a person. Remember his students will all tell you that their instructor is the best thing since Bruce Lee; you find out for yourself if he is or not. Once you have made your choice put your heart and soul into it. In my Dojo hangs a banner with the inscription 'ICHI KO – ICHI SHIN' this means One Heart – One Mind, and it implies that if you are to be truly successful in anything you must put your whole heart (body) and mind (intelect) into the pursuit of that goal; in this case Karate. You cannot spread yourself out doing other things and still hope to get a deep understanding of Karate.

To go one step further I would like to present to you the history of the two forms of Karate I am familiar with, and along the way hopefully show the differences that exist between them. Although I studied Tani-Ha Shito-ryu for ten years before coming to Goju-ryu, I would like to give you the history of the Goju-ryu first as this is the older of the two and indeed as you will see was one of the 'Parents' as it were, of Mr. Tani's Karate.

Goju-ryu as we know it today was formulated by Miyagi Chojun Sensei. He was born in Naha the capital city of Okinawa on the 25th April 1888. His family were wealthy and belonged to the upper class of Okinawan society. His family had a shipping business which specialised in importing medicines from China. When just eleven years old he was introduced to Karate. His first instructor was Aragaki Ryuko Sensei, and for most of his early years' training he concentrated on Hojo-Undo to build himself up. When he was fourteen years old the young Miyagi Chojun was introduced to Higaonna Kanryo Sensei who was at that time the leading Karate Master on all Okinawa.

It was hoped by Aragaki Sensei that his young pupil would be taken on by Master Higaonna. However there were many more people trying to train with Master Higaonna than he wanted to teach. For Higaonna Sensei had a very strict form of training, and new students were required to do menial tasks for a considerable length of time before receiving Karate instruction. This was in keeping with the traditions of China where Master Higaonna learned his art. Though it may be easy to look back now and see Miyagi Sensei as some kind of perfect Karate master with incredible powers it is well to

111

remember that several times it is said he doubted as to whether he would carry on with his training. The fact that he did, as has my Sensei, and yours, is proof that the tough time you are going through at the moment has been experienced by many of us. We came through, so can you.

Karate training in those days consisted of mainly Kata practice. Repeated over and over many hundreds of times the Kata became the anvil on which the person's character was forged. There are many stories of the severity of the training Master Miyagi underwent in order to learn his Karate. Sometimes he had to hold himself so firm in the execution of Sanchin kata that he would faint from the continual effort. Stories are legion about the old days on Okinawa; suffice it to say that through the efforts of men such as Miyagi Sensei we now have this wonderful thing we call Karate-do. After fifteen years together the student and master were separated only by death. The death of Higaonna Kanryo Sensei was a mighty blow to Mayagi Sensei however he knew that his Master had entrusted him to carry on and to develop his precious legacy.

Miyagi Sensei travelled to China and in the same place where Master Higaonna had trained he studied for a short time. On his return to Okinawa, Sensei Miyagi formulated three new kata, Tensho, Gekisai Dai-ichi and Gekisai Dai-ni. The former is perhaps the physical epitaph to Miyagi Sensei. The latter two kata were officially adopted by Goju-ryu in the early forties and have remained as the two 'beginners' to this day.

Throughout his life Sensei Miyagi saw his training as a way of life. He saw it as a way of achieving peace and tranquility within himself. The term Go translates as hard, Ju as gentle. In calling his method of Karate by this name he was teaching that all things are made whole by the coming together of the two opposites. Let me try to explain in modern terms what I mean by this. In all things there is an opposite, Day/Night, Big/Small, Fast/Slow, Hard/Soft. If you know only one side of something then really you do not know anything. How do you describe to a person who has always been blind how bright the day is? He will never understand what you mean for he has only ever known the dark. What Sensei Miyagi wanted people to understand was that one should live one's life with this in mind and not live only on one side. People get upset if they fail at something in life and this can lead to bad behaviour, crime, etc. But how can they enjoy success if they have not known the pain of failure? Miyagi Sensei believed that through the hard physical training, over the years the body would grow strong and hard while at the same time the character would soften and become gentle. Having achieved the two sides of hardness and softness within himself the person was then in a position to live a contented and productive life unaffected by the petty squabbles that afflict the minds and bodies of untrained people. Also he felt that through the lessons learnt during Karate training a person could cope better with the trials of life itself.

Miyagi Sensei himself had many devastating moments in his life and during the battle of Okinawa in the second world war he lost his son and also his top student. He did not teach Karate during those dark days on Okinawa, however in 1946 he was appointed a director of the Civil Association for Physical Education. He began to teach Karate again at the Police Training Academy on Okinawa. It was said that during the war the new recruits to the Japanese army that came from Okinawa were in the main stronger and better in physique than the average Japanese recruits. This was because many Okinawans did Karate training as part of their physical education at school. Before the war Okinawan Karate spread to Japan and very quickly grew in popularity. At that time Karate Masters were in great demand and some of the house-

113

hold names in Karate of today made their way to mainland Japan and started to teach Karate on a full time basis. Such people as Funakoshi Gichin Sensei, and Mabuni Kenwa Sensei. Also at this time Miyagi Sensei travelled to Japan to answer the many requests to teach his art. However Sensei Miyagi never spent a great deal of time in Japan and never stayed there for longer than a couple of months at a time. He did however spend some time in the Hawaiian Islands. In fact he spent ten months there touring the islands and teaching Goju-ryu Karate-do. Sensei Miyagi always impressed on his students that the purpose of Karate training was to build a strong character, and he himself was a living example of the results obtainable through constant and diligent Karate training. It is said that his power was awesome and yet it is well known that he was a true gentleman in every sense. Indeed on Okinawa he was and still is known as 'Bushi' Miyagi. Bushi on Okinawa means that you are a noble warrior, similar to the knight in shining armour in the Europe of old. It meant that though capable of great power the person was good and just, true and honest. Miyagi Sensei was certainly all these things.

The emphasis, as much as I am aware of any, that I have found in Goju-ryu Karate-do is that of building character. The physical training is very tough and demanding, and here one could say the emphasis is on the coordination of breathing with physical movement. To achieve a kind of harmony between one's thoughts and one's actions. The techniques of Goju-ryu Karate manifest themselves as either hard strong techniques such as punching or elbow striking. Other techniques, such as blocking appear as relaxed and subtle moves. As with any form of Karate it takes many years of real training to understand and master these ideas, nevertheless this is possible for all of us to achieve; all we have to do is work hard for many years and we will achieve our own conquests within Karate and in life.

As one can see from this short history of the founder of Goju-ryu his Karate has a deep and profound nature. At first it might seem a contradiction that such concepts should come from a fighting system known throughout the world for its lethal effectiveness. But it is exactly the trials, failures, and successes that one goes through during the study of Goju-ryu that forges a person's mind and therefore nature into that of a decent and honest member of society.

Tani-ha Shito-ryu or Shukokai as the organisation is called, is based very firmly on mathematical and scientific principles. Although some say that Tani Sensei devised his style of Karate specifically for sport, I personally feel this is a drastic over simplification of the truth.

Sensei Tani was born in Kobe Japan in 1921. He began to study Karate as a young boy whilst still at school. His first taste of Karate was Goju-ryu, and he occasionally trained directly under Master Miyagi. At the age of nineteen he entered Doshisha University in Kyoto and there contined to train in Karate at the university Karate club. This club however was of the Shito-ryu style of Karate and was directed by the founder of Shito-ryu Master Mabuni Kenawa. Mabuni Sensei also had ties with Goju-ryu, for back on his native Okinawa Mabuni Sensei had trained for many years under Master Higaonna Kanryo Sensei who was the Sensei of Master Miyagi. In fact the two men were friends for many years.

In 1948 Sensei Tani opened his own dojo and called it the Shukokai. He was already looking further into Karate than he had learnt from the Shito-ryu system. After touring South Africa with his close friend and fellow Karate-ka Fujiwara Sensei they began to wonder what would be necessary for a small Japanese to develop the same power the huge South Africans had. So they looked to the physical laws applied in sports such as golf, athletics, and swimming. The laws of Newton came in very handy and I can well remember learning that Mass + Acceleration = Force. This basic principle or law of physics was applied to all our punches and kicks. Emphasis was very much on bodyweight distribution to enhance speed and therefore power. I can also remember vividly being impressed by the story of the bullet. It goes as follows.

A bullet is just a small piece of metal right. So if I throw it at your chest as hard as I can it will just bounce off and do you no harm. However if I shoot that same bullet at you from a gun it will surely kill you. So what is the difference? Well, only the speed has changed. The speed being much greater when the bullet left the gun gives the small piece of metal a lethal force.

Quite convincing isn't it, and so it should be because it's true. Shukokai has been called 'Logical' and even 'Scientific' Karate. The emphasis as I saw it whilst studying the system was on speed of movement and economy of action. The speed and dynamic use of one's body suits I feel the young and athletic best. While I was with the Shukokai, little if any time was spent discussing the furthering of ones mental state. Hard work it indeed was, but it lacked for me, and I stress for me, something that I was looking for in Karate. In the last few years training with the Shukokai I did get to taste the things I was looking for. This was because of the conversations I had with Tomiyama Sensei. I should point out that the decision to stop training with the Shukokai and Tomiyama Sensei in particular was for me a very traumatic experience. It took a long time, many months in fact, to face up to the fact that for me the way of Shito-ryu was wrong. Even as I write these words my loyalty and feelings for Tomiyama Sensei make me hesitate, but I know I am right in the way I am training. Higaonna Morio Sensei is the embodiment of all that I want to be through Karate training. He is not a god, I do not adore him, but my admiration and respect for him have no boundary. I have seen at first hand how he lives his quiet and humble life. I feel that he above anyone I have ever met has come closest to the ideal of a Karate man.

Author (1) with Terry O'Neill Sensei at a course in Devon in 1986.

The author, feeling good, at a park entrance,
after three weeks in Okinawa.

Christina Larsen, 2nd dan, doing 'Sepai' kata.

Epilogue

So there it is. Of course my life goes on and so does my training. I feel my Karate training has completed one of it's many circles. I believe I have found my own way within Karate-do, the way of Goju-Ryu.

It is not the right way nor the wrong way, it is simply my way. I have found peace and real contentment in my practice. My nature and the way I deal with the problems in my life have altered considerably since I first entered a dojo and put on a gi. I feel I have made a little progress along the path that is Karate-Do, I also know I have a long way further to go, but I have met a man who in my opinion has gained real mastery of himself through hard and diligent training in Karate.

I should like to make it clear though that it is the level of Karate in Higaonna Sensei that I admire and not just the man. Though I respect him very greatly for having the personal strength and true courage to follow the way of Karate-Do so thoroughly, for it is not the easiest way of life, and although many pay lip service to it, very few practice Karate outside the dojo.

It is to this end that I am working, to fill myself with the concepts of Karate-Do.

Remember the finger pointing at the moon.

Tomiyama Sensei with the author and students at the
Stockport Bushido Kan. Terry Harrison is in the centre.

(Left to right) Tommy Rowe, author, Lee Rowe (Tommy's
son), Steve O'Driscale, at the Jin-Sei-Do dojo
(way of life dojo).

Tomiyama Keiji Sensei at the author's Stockport dojo.

Sensei and author at Higaonna dojo, 1984.

Kina Sensei, 10th Dan, at the Kina dojo, Okinawa, 1984.

123

Michael Ch'ing, Chief Instructor for Goju-ryu in Malaysia, at the Higaonna dojo in Okinawa.

Suzuki Sensei with the author at Pepinster, Belgium, 1978
Suzuki Sensei was 7th dan at this time.

Training with the 'Chi-ishi'.

125

A movement from 'Saiyunchin' kata.

Author training in the 'Saifa' kata.

Technique from 'Saiyunchin' kata.

Dave Moss Sensei, 4th dan, instructor to the Channel Islands, with the author.